Reading the New Testament

Reading the New Testament is intended as a companion volume to the successful New Testament Readings series. It analyses the many ways in which the New Testament can be read and interpreted.

Rather than prescribing one 'correct' way of reading, this study offers an overview of and introduction to the most influential theories of recent scholarship, discussing the background against which such theories are developed. It shows the advantages of combining methods of reading, thus stimulating an interaction between various approaches, illustrated by the individual volumes in the series.

This is an important addition to New Testament literature, offering the student of religion a comprehensive overview of the methods and approaches used by scholars in the field. As such, it will make invaluable reading not just for the student, but for anyone interested in an introduction to this fascinating area of religious and literary thought.

John M. Court has taught biblical studies at the University of Kent for more than twenty years. He is the author of two volumes on the Book of Revelation and co-author of *The New Testament World*.

New Testament Readings
Edited by John M. Court
University of Kent at Canterbury

Reading the
New Testament

John M. Court

London and New York

First published 1997
by Routledge
11 New Fetter Lane, London EC4P 4EE
Simultaneously published in the USA and Canada
by Routledge
29 West 35th Street, New York, NY 10001

© 1997 John M. Court

Typeset in Garamond by
LaserScript Limited, Mitcham, Surrey
Printed and bound in Great Britain by
Clays Ltd, St. Ives PLC

British Library Cataloguing in Publication Data
A catalogue record for this book is available from the British Library

Library of Congress Cataloging in Publication Data
Court, John M.
  Reading the New Testament/John M. Court.
    p. cm. – (New Testament readings)
  Includes bibliographical references and index.
  1. Bible. N.T. – Reading. 2. Bible. N.T. – Criticism, interpretation, etc.
I. Title. II. Series.
BS2361.2.C675 1997
225.6'01 – dc20   96–33159
                                             CIP

ISBN 0–415–10367–3
ISBN 0–415–10368–1 (pbk)

To the memory of
ELSIE DORIS COURT

'Master, now you are dismissing your servant in peace'
(Luke 2.29)

Contents

Preface

This volume belongs with the Routledge series *New Testament Readings* as a companion volume. Its aim is to suggest and to illustrate a range of ways in which the New Testament may be read and interpreted. It is certainly not prescribing one single way in which the New Testament must be read. If there is a tactic inherent in the arrangement of both this volume and the series, it is to suggest the advantages of combining methods of reading, stimulating an interaction between various approaches. Individual volumes in the series have already illustrated, and will continue to illustrate, how this can be done.

Inevitably the illustrations and emphases of this present volume are time-bound, belonging in a certain era. Just as the base camp of the explorer Captain Robert Scott, with all its provisions and equipment, remains frozen in the Antarctic at the date of his second expedition in 1912, so this volume cannot avoid reflecting those attitudes to biblical interpretation which are beginning to prevail in the United Kingdom in the middle years of the 1990s. Some attempt will be made to indicate how we reached this point, and where we might go from here, but the task of this book is fundamentally to describe and discuss where we are. I am far from suggesting that definitive conclusions have been reached; there is still much exploration to be undertaken, and lessons to be learnt for other times and places.

A deliberate decision has been taken in this volume to avoid the technical discussion of hermeneutical principles and theories, in favour of describing the methods at work. The reader who would like to proceed further in studying theory should consult the primary writers, figures such as Barthes, Derrida, Eco, Gadamer, Greimas, Lacan, Lévi-Strauss, Ricoeur, de Saussure, or make use of good secondary surveys, such as those by Anthony Thiselton.

In terms of the immediate readership, envisaged as I write, this volume has a twofold intention. Firstly, I am challenged to respond to the suggestion made by Richard Stoneman, the senior editor of Routledge, that the series *New Testament Readings* should have a companion volume, outlining especially the new ways of reading the New Testament documents. I owe a debt of gratitude to Richard and his team at Routledge for the superb presentation of the series and for the tireless encouragement of me as series editor. It seems entirely appropriate that the series editor should write the companion volume, not only to keep me on my toes, but also to ensure that the approach matches the general intentions of the series.

Secondly, I hope to meet the need for a more accessible general introduction to the ways of approaching the New Testament text, suitable for student use. One might have thought that there was already an abundance of introductions to the New Testament, some of which even are still in print. But I was encouraged personally in my aims by a number of good friends and academic colleagues; in particular I am grateful to Andrew Lincoln of the Biblical Studies Department at Sheffield University for his advice that there is a real need for an accessible guide for students on how to begin. My volume derives in large part from the experience of teaching at the University of Kent an introductory course for first-year students (general humanities, not specialist theology) on how to read the Bible. To those groups also I would want to express my thanks.

John M. Court
May 1996

Acknowledgements

I would like to express my sincere thanks to all who have provided encouragement, advice, suggestions and materials in the preparation of this volume. In particular I am grateful to Ingrid Rosa Kitzberger, James Resseguie and Bas Van Iersel, materials from whose unpublished work are included here with due acknowledgement. A special vote of thanks is due to Professor Frank Kermode of the University of Cambridge, and to Professor Leslie Houlden of King's College, London for their respective encouragement of this series and this volume.

I wish to express thanks to the Revd Nigel Guthrie, Chaplain and Information Officer, and to Mrs Connie Downes, an archivist, both of Coventry Cathedral, and also to the Revd Stephen Twycross, priest in charge of St John Baptist, Stokesay, Shropshire, and to the Revd Trevor Pitt, vicar of Elham in Kent, for their invaluable assistance in preparing the subject matter used for chapter 9 (Texts as Slogans).

Strenuous efforts have been made by author and publisher to secure copyright permissions from all the appropriate copyright holders. Particular acknowledgements are here made to the following:

Mike Kidd of Biff Products for the cartoon on p. 61.

The Revd Professor Jerome Murphy O'Connor of Ecole Biblique, Jerusalem for the two archaeological plans on pp. 99, 100.

SPCK and the Editors of *Theology* for the reproduction of the Postscript.

Jonathan Fisher and Lion Educational for 'The Long Silence' (pp. 125–6).

Faber and Faber with Richard Hamer as translator for the poetry on pp. xiii–xiv and Faber and Faber with the estate of Wallace Stevens for the poem on p. 159.

Penguin Books and the estate of Edmund Crispin (Bruce Montgomery) for pp. 20f.

The author and publishers will be glad to hear from other holders of copyright, not so far identified or contacted, so that due and grateful acknowledgement may be made in any subsequent edition.

A Bible riddle

This eighth-century Saxon riddle – the solution to which is the Bible itself – serves to show that there is more than one way of looking at these texts. The reader may be arrested by the external appearance of the volume itself, and is likely also to be interested in how it came to be, but will ultimately concentrate on the subject-matter and its meaning, or variety of meanings.

> Some enemy deprived me of my life
> And took away my worldly strength, then wet me,
> Dipped me in water, took me out again,
> Set me in sunshine, where I quickly lost
> The hairs I had. Later the knife's hard edge
> Cut me with all impurities ground off.
> Then fingers folded me; the bird's fine raiment
> Traced often over me with useful drops
> Across my brown domain, swallowed the tree-dye
> Mixed up with water, stepped on me again
> Leaving dark tracks. The hero clothed me then
> With boards to guard me, stretched hide over me,
> Decked me with gold; and thus the splendid work
> Of smiths, with wire bound round, embellished me.
> Now my red dye and all my decorations,
> My gorgeous trappings far and wide proclaim
> The Lord of Hosts, not grief for foolish sins.
> If sons of men will make good use of me,
> By that they shall be sounder, more victorious,
> Their hearts more bold, their minds more full of joy,
> Their spirits wiser; they shall have more friends,
> Dear ones and kinsmen, truer and more good,

More kind and faithful, who will add more glory
And happiness by favours, who will lay
Upon them kindnesses and benefits,
And clasp them fast in the embrace of love.
Say who I am, useful to men. My name
Is famous, good to men, and also sacred.

(Translated by Richard Hamer)

Introduction: On reading the Bible

The first necessity is to establish a definition of the subject with which this book is concerned. This may at first sight seem so obvious a question and answer as to be virtually redundant. We know what the Bible is, and we can find the New Testament within it, and thanks to widespread literacy we know how to read. But if we probe a little deeper, some of the complexities of the question will emerge. And therefore the answer will take a little longer! What then is the Bible – or more particularly the New Testament – which we are reading?

The questioning starts with the English translation which we have on the bookshelf, or beside us, as we read this introduction. Is it a classic translation such as the Authorised or King James's Version? Or is it one of a multiplicity of modern translations? I would not want to suggest that any one translation is perfect, or that any other translations are automatically unreliable. Some scholars, however, will point to the vast range of new linguistic and historical evidence that has appeared since 1611. Other critics will argue about the deficiencies of some modern usage of the English language, for the purposes of accurate translation. But if you compare several versions or use something like *The Complete Parallel Bible* (Oxford University Press, 1993), this will rapidly show you how different are the possibilities of translation. So which Bible – whose New Testament – are we reading?

Let us suppose that in the historical quest for precision and reliability the reader goes by way of the translations and the earliest Latin and Syriac texts back to the original languages, the Hebrew and Aramaic of the Old Testament, or the *Koine* or Common Greek of the New Testament. It is impossible to find a first edition, as one might expect to do for a modern novel. There are no autographs (i.e. manuscripts from the pen of New Testament writers); there are no rough drafts or author's notebooks to guide us to the writer's first intentions.

For the New Testament the first manuscripts are fragments of papyrus scrolls from the early second century CE and onwards, or the major codices (texts in book form) which date back to the fourth century at the earliest. Even when dealing with the early texts in New Testament Greek there is plentiful scope for a variety of readings. There is no single text of the New Testament of which it can be said with confidence: 'This is the point of reference, this is the Bible.' Some enthusiasts will argue for the early Syriac translations as providing a way back to the earliest Palestinian traditions about Jesus. But there can be no certainty and any reader (whether a scholar or not) must face the facts of a pluralism of texts and a variety of possible readings.

The position is no more straightforward for readers of the Old Testament. If anything, the gap is much larger between the era of the first writers and the dates of the earliest manuscripts, although the biblical texts among the scrolls from the Dead Sea have narrowed the gap significantly. What can be said for certain in scientific, or archaeological, or literary terms is just this: 'the Scriptures' which Jesus read and expounded are not exactly identifiable with any agreed collection of holy books of his day, nor are they identical with the editions of the Hebrew Bible which are available today. Once again the reader has to be reconciled to the idea of a plurality of Bibles.

The definition of the limits (or canon) of the Old or New Testaments represents a much later stage in those historical processes by which the idea of Scripture has evolved. If the concept of canon is appropriate to the Hebrew Bible – and this is disputed – it can only have become a full reality, in terms of the threefold collection of Law, Prophets and Writings (see Luke 24.44), at or after the meeting of the Pharisaic Rabbis (the reconstituted Sanhedrin) at Jamnia, which followed the fall of the Jerusalem temple in 70 CE.

The canon of the New Testament only achieves fixity in the fourth century CE, following a succession of scholarly debates and the political moves of councils of the Church. The earliest steps towards defining such limits seem to have been taken in the second century, in response to controversy. One of the first pressures on the Church was a kind of prototype canon, or approved body of texts, proposed by Marcion, the son of the bishop of Sinope, who was expelled from the Church at Rome about 144 CE. His choice of texts was in support of his own beliefs, rejecting the Old Testament and its influences; this left him with a truncated form of Luke's Gospel (minus the infancy stories) and the letters of Paul. Another pressure came from the wide-ranging debates about the boundaries of orthodoxy and heresy, particularly with regard to Gnostic groups within and outside of the Christian movement, who placed special emphasis on revelatory texts and sources of 'knowledge' to ensure personal salvation. A third pressure resulted from a fresh upsurge of Christian prophecy; a second-century movement called Montanism claimed a continuity of direct, charismatic inspiration within the Church. Could one then accept that the first-century Gospels constituted any final form of revelation?

To talk like this of a canon or collection of texts draws our attention to an obvious fact about the New Testament (even more so the Bible). These texts are not a unity, like integrated chapters in a single volume. They are more like an anthology, or a collection of essays, on a rather broad theme. A fierce critic might ask whether the Bible is a book or a ragbag, a totality or merely a repository. It is a question about the relative value of individual stories on the one hand, and any overall shape, or overriding themes and 'message', on the other. Even those commonplace references to the Bible as a 'library' themselves acknowledge the fact of pluralism, and draw attention to the variety of literary genres to be found within this collection.

Frank Kermode summarised the issues involved in the description of the 'Bible library':

> The Bible is a collection of ancient writings, and, except to believers in plenary inspiration, it is a rather random, mis-cellaneous, and fortuitous compilation. It is possible to regard it as in some sense a unity, but that unity has been imposed by history, by the fact that its parts have coexisted and been interpreted together for so long. If the early Christian bishop Marcion had had his way in the second century there would not be an Old Testament in Christian Bibles. But for good or ill the Old Testament has been, formidably and formatively, in the Bible. And the constituent books are not quite the same as they would have been if each had survived in isolation.
>
> Of course this is to say a great deal less than that, bound

together, they offer the one essential reference book, a complete guide to conduct, private and public, as well as to salvation. Yet the notion that they did so – the Old Testament no less than the New – was generally assumed by the communities that accepted Reform in the sixteenth century, and it prevailed until late in the next.

> The Book of Books;
> On which who looks,
> As he should do aright, shall never need
> Wish for a better light
> To guide him in the night . . .

So the poet Christopher Harvey.

(Kermode, 1994, p. 4)

The majority of the twenty-seven books of the New Testament are letters and sermons from Church leaders to individuals, congregations or the Catholic Church. There are four Gospels, apparently chosen to represent unity in diversity, if Irenaeus's words about four Gospels for the four winds or four corners of the earth are to be taken seriously. Then there is a document of Church history, the Acts of the Apostles (principally Peter and Paul), and a bizarre visionary document about Christian experience in the first century, the Christian Apocalypse or Book of Revelation.

Therefore, at least in our modern context, for us to define a particular New Testament text that is being read would entail defining one literary genre out of a number within the collection, where that collection itself represents one of a number of options in combining of texts, out of a pluralism of possible traditions in various stages of development. In fact there has never been one Bible text which all readers could hold in common and regard as standard.

The next question to be asked concerns the object of our reading, in the sense of our objectives in reading, our purpose for wishing to read. Here too it is necessary to analyse the situation and indicate the possibilities. Again, to give this question a comparative perspective, I should like to refer to a little pamphlet, written by Alan Richardson, entitled *How To Read The Bible – with Special Reference to the Old Testament*. This was published in January 1943 by the Church Information Board, Westminster, for the price of 6d (or 2.5p). Richardson stressed how important it was to use the method of reading appropriate to one's reasons for wanting to read. He asked, 'Why should we read the Bible?' and offered three possible answers:

1 as Great literature and because of its literary influence;
2 for Spiritual, moral and religious consolation;
3 as the Record of the evolution of man's religious hopes and beliefs.

The polarising questions would be: Is the Bible our noblest thoughts about God, or God's message to us? Are there other works with which the Bible is comparable, or does it have a unique status?

If we say that the Bible is uniquely God's revelation to us, then, Richardson asked, are we bound to be 'fundamentalist' in our attitude to the text? Would any critical discrimination amount to tampering with divine revelation? Or does the 'inspiration' of the Bible consist in prophetic insights into the way God acts in history, in the fact that these have been validated in experience, and in the consequent understanding that humanity has gained of God's will? Does this mean that there are different levels of inspirational value in different texts of the Bible, according to the degree in which, for example, prophetic insight is revealed?

Fifty years after Alan Richardson set out these questions, how does this compare with the prevailing options and perspectives of the 1990s? Can our modern mode of reading ever be one of submission to the text as the complete answer to all our problems? To adopt Christopher Harvey's poetic words

> The Book of Books;
> On which who looks,
> As he should do aright, shall never need
> Wish for a better light
> To guide him in the night . . .

at the end of the twentieth century might be regarded as the Christian equivalent of extreme Islamic fundamentalism. Even inside most Christian communities is not the prevailing way of reading much more selective and discriminating, as well as more open, interactive and participatory?

Bible studies in Church groups have been radically affected in recent years by a variety of independent influences:

1 new theories about adult learning and experiential education;
2 liberation theology (among different kinds of oppressed peoples) which emphasises practical exegesis of the Bible in the community;
3 anti-intellectual revolts in Western society, reacting against academic traditions;
4 rediscovery of Christian spirituality in the Western Churches.

The results of these pressures are extremely uneven and very diverse. Among the leading writers and guides on the subject are Hans-Ruedi Weber, Walter Wink and Walter Hollenweger. As Chris Peck writes:

> Weber sees the text as being the product of a creative, imaginative, oral tradition and so his methods use story telling, drawing and music. . . . Wink sees the text as an individually transforming force and so his methods focus on ways of enabling participants to get inside themselves, while Hollenweger sees the text as the result of a process of editing over hundreds of years, produced within a particular sociological context, and so his methods try to make the fruit of critical scholarship available to participants through complex productions.
>
> (1988, p. 31)

There is a potential here for revolutionising the traditionally religious study of the Bible:

> people who have either been alienated from the Bible, or who have not had access to it, becoming engaged in and excited about Bible study, in a way which leads to their being challenged to act differently in their lives, and the potential for groups and small communities to engage together with the Bible.
>
> (ibid. p. 35)

But such activist approaches – both individual and collective – should not obscure the fact that each of the leading practitioners operates with quite different presuppositions about the fundamental nature of the Bible and the means of interaction. It is interesting to ask whether these modern attitudes to the Bible, far from being a fundamentalist submission to the text, are actually more pro-active than re-active.

But the present author is not wishing to assume that his readers are either Christians or potential Christian converts challenged by the Bible. Alan Richardson in 1943 recognised other motivations for reading the Bible among students of literature or historians of ideas. Today even these options are not exhaustive. There must be almost as many reasons for reading as there are readers. I have no wish to categorise people, but only to ask readers why they are reading and whether the methods they use are appropriate to their aims.

There is now available at least one interactive computer game, based on compact discs, that permits the player to rewrite the Bible, identify with Judas Iscariot, or colour the narrative to create a black Christ. This seems to go beyond what a Church spokesperson meant when responding to the news that a Nintendo Gameboy would be placed alongside the Gideon Bible in hotel bedrooms:

> The Word of God is for everybody. Nintendo isn't. Anyway the Bible is far more interactive than any video game.

With the interactive compact discs, produced by the aptly named Fatal Media, the death of Christ on the cross can be made to depend on a keyboard manipulation: Jesus can die sooner, later, or never; he can even marry Mary Magdalene.

This is an extreme – probably a grotesque – example of a general principle that must be taken seriously when considering how the Bible should be read in the 1990s. *Everyone interprets the Bible in their own way.* There is much overlap, but no two people will see it in exactly the same way. This is as true for the general reader as it is in the competing methods of biblical scholars, or on the battle-ground between religious parties, liberal or conservative.

Independence in interpretation is a positive principle. But it has its negative side. An immediate anxiety is whether there is then any common ground for shared understanding about the text. In an age of postmodernism dominated by deconstruction, are we left with no way of evaluating any given interpretation? In short, does anything go? Is one person's guess about meaning as good as another's because nobody can claim to speak of *the* meaning?

The academic profession of biblical scholars certainly still works on the assumption that some interpretations of a particular text are better than others. Biblical scholarship is today a fiercely competitive world, like much else in the late twentieth century, with a changing canon of interpretations. But it is possible that there might yet be some broad principles of exegesis, some forum of debate about the relative value of different methods, some agenda for hermeneutics seen in an inclusive rather than exclusive spirit. The optimist might hope that this would lead to mutual enlightenment among scholars and cooperation between readers.

If one asks, in a tentative and hopeful way, where textual meaning is to be found, there are at present three answers which might be given. To set them out at this stage will give us an opportunity to compare the answers and analyse them. It will be the business of this book to do precisely this as we investigate the working methods which lead to such answers, and further our discussion of how to read the New Testament. It is possible to identify meaning in three places:

1 Meaning is found *behind* a text – that is, in the historical background to the text and its sources. The text acts as a window through which we look at what lies beyond.
2 Meaning is found *in* a text – that is, in the interaction of elements and structures which exist within the final form of a text. The text is thus like a specimen slide placed under a microscope.
3 Meaning is found *in front of* a text, in the sense that the construction of meaning takes place in the interaction between the text and the reader. The text acts as a mirror in which we see ourselves; the meaningful text lies between us and the visible text. The activity resembles 'reading between the lines'.

Chapter 1

Historical reading

> What it had been was history. What it was to be was not history at all.
>
> Alan Bennett, *Writing Home*

A treasured painting in the National Gallery's collection is a panel with an unusual depiction of the entombment of Christ. Although *The Entombment* was purchased as being the work of Michelangelo, the attribution has been disputed periodically and the work assigned to a lesser Florentine artist, a contemporary called Baccio Bandinelli. Even among those who maintain it is by Michelangelo there is no consensus about the painting's date. It was painted in Florence in his twentieth year, or in Rome when he was thirty-one, or later still when he was aged forty. This argument is often based on the fashion of the clothes or hairstyles in the painting.

This is a good example of a historical enquiry, where every conceivable clue from external and internal evidence is examined in order to 'place' the subject; but in the end there are at least four divergent but sustainable conclusions. It reminds one of the problems posed by the evidence of the Gospels about the dates of Jesus' life and how old he was. Luke 3.23 held that Jesus was 'about thirty years of age' when his ministry began with his baptism by John. But according to John 8.57, the Jews alluded to his age as 'not yet fifty years old'. Are both ages to be taken literally? Could both be correct? There is discrepancy here, but not necessarily incompatibility (unless, like Irenaeus you take John 8.57 to imply that Jesus was forty-nine years of age – which is the age of perfect maturity, being seven times the seven ages of man!).

According to Matthew's Gospel (2.1, 19) Jesus was born in the final year of King Herod's reign (4 BCE). The birth stories in the

Gospels of Matthew and Luke concur in very few details; the only points of direct agreement are that Jesus was born from a virgin mother in Bethlehem, and that his parents' names were Joseph and Mary. But Luke also says that John the Baptist was born in Herod's reign and that Mary's child Jesus would be born approximately six months after Elizabeth's son John (Luke 1.5, 26). If Jesus was 'about thirty' (Luke 3.1, 23), in the fifteenth year of Tiberius's reign as emperor of Rome (29/28 CE), this information is roughly compatible with a birth date in 4 BCE.

The real problem comes with Luke's reference to the birth of Christ at the time of the census when Quirinius was governor of Syria (2.1f). In the words of Robin Lane Fox:

> According to Josephus [the Jewish historian] Quirinius was governor of Syria with authority over Judaea in AD 6, when the province was brought under direct Roman control. The year was a critical moment in Jewish history, as important to its province as the year of 1972 to Northern Ireland, the start of direct rule.
>
> (1991, p. 28)

The result of this historical investigation seems to be that Luke offers two dates for Jesus' birth, ten years apart.

The effect is similar to the disputes about the painting in the National Gallery. One detail of the picture has caused the dating to be shifted by ten years. Has historical criticism betrayed a serious inconsistency in Luke's Gospel? Does it mean that one cannot trust this 'fact' about Jesus' birth, or the rest of the Gospel data, as in the usual sense historical? The result seems to be what Christian readers in particular have dreaded about historical criticism: that it undermines the essentials of the faith. The strange thing to observe, however, about Robin Lane Fox's approach is that, while he demolishes Luke's dating of the Nativity, he supports what the fourth Gospel says about Jesus' age because (according to Fox) the author was John the Apostle and therefore a primary witness.

We need to look more closely at what historical criticism involves. Our example of Jesus' age and date of birth has entailed comparing three New Testament Gospels and two synoptic Gospels, with one another and with John. But the critical process has also taken reference points from outside the Bible, dates of kings and emperors and the writings of ancient historians. Such external comparisons are not the easy (and definitive) matter they might seem, for several reasons.

Ancient historians (such as Tacitus, Josephus and the author of the Acts of the Apostles) do not make a practice of coordinating their data with one another, as modern historians do. Cross-references do not exist (although Luke 3.1 makes an attempt). There is also a problem with the calendar – more strictly with calendars; for there were several and they ran from different points in the year. The Jewish calendar at this period started in the spring, the Macedonian in the autumn, and the Julian (the Roman solar calendar initiated by Julius Caesar) in midwinter. Ancient dates were often given by the years of office of a monarch or governor; how do such dates intersect with calendar years, when periods of office start at different times? And finally there is an obvious difference between the inclusive and exclusive methods of reckoning intervals of time. For the Roman, the day after tomorrow, forty-eight hours' time, would be three days away, because he counted today as day one. All of these factors must create a degree of imprecision for the historian today. There is more than one way of calculating the fifteenth year of the Emperor Tiberius!

But the matter is more difficult still. We take a standard dating system of day/month/complete year for granted. But such dates only became common in England around 1500 CE (the Common or Christian Era). The explicitly Christian numbering of years AD (Anno Domini, or in the year of the Lord) was introduced by Dionysius Exiguus in AD 525 (or 525 CE, as we would now say, more neutrally). But it was not until the Gregorian calendar of 1582 CE that the beginning of the year on 1 January was established for all time, prospectively and retrospectively (although still not for all cultures). Then began the long process of converting older datings to the new style.

We have little problem with standard dating, so long as we remember to write it down at the time! But any retrospective dating must open up margins of error. In recollection we can lengthen or foreshorten a period of time. We may transpose the order of events, or assign them to different years, unless we can tie them securely (and accurately?) to a particularly memorable event. Robin Lane Fox obviously places trust in such a linkage when he emphasises Josephus's evidence on the date of Quirinius. But is this Jewish/Roman association of events really any more (or less) reliable than the links made by the Christian/Graeco-Roman writer Luke?

The moral is that we need to be hyper-cautious about conclusions from any ancient historical evidence, sacred or secular.

Allowances must be made for the problems of chronology, and perhaps even more so for the interpretation of events in all kinds of meaningful and symbolic ways, and overall for the essentially ideological motivations for history-writing in the ancient world (in contrast to the scientific controls on modern historiography). The harsh truth is that there is very little continuity in the idea of 'history' (the purposes and methods of writing history) between then and now. This is why we have problems with the lack of firm information from Luke about the time of Jesus' birth, or for that matter about the circumstances of Paul's death, at the opposite end of this two-volume work. We find it difficult to conceive that a history would ever have been written that did not start by recounting such essential 'facts' straightforwardly. But of course there is the question whether the Christian movement had any sort of 'archives' and how one could possibly have discovered such facts at the time. Apart from this practical reason, Luke's outlook surely must have been much closer in chronology and ideology to the classical historians of ancient Greece and Rome than to the modern scientific historian.

The classical historians Thucydides and Livy both wrote history in the interests of moral and political causes; Tacitus did also, combining it with a critical, satirical vein. For us it is probably better to 'enter into the spirit' of what it meant to write a historical record in the ancient world, rather than tinker with Luke's wording and thereby free him from the accusation of error. Although it is true that Luke 2.2 *might* be read as saying: 'This census was before the one Quirinius held . . .', it is much more likely that his information was either confused or inadequate by modern historical standards of evidence.

Even if this debate is pursued as far as possible, so that the issue may be resolved, in terms of what are margins of error satisfactory for ancient history, or perhaps by making improvements in the accuracy of the text, a larger question still remains. Does Luke intend to make historical statements in a matter of fact way? Or is the detail of his text intentionally symbolic?

Jesus is born at the turning point of the Roman world, when it is taking stock of itself. As his ministry begins Jesus is at the optimum age of human vigour – thirty years. In the future, some apocalyptic traditions will imagine the ideal state of the after-life when everybody is aged thirty! Is John's tradition of Jesus being 'not yet fifty' a symbolic reference to the nearness of the biblical Jubilee

$(7 \times 7 = 49)$ when the whole world is renewed after the ultimate sabbath rest? Or is the age range represented by the two traditions (Luke's and John's), that is, between thirty and fifty, an echo of the proper age-qualification in order to hold religious office, as we see this echoed in the documents of the Jewish sect at Qumran? It is very difficult to set limits to, or gauge the plausibility of, such symbolic – as opposed to historical – intentions. In an ideological style of history-writing it is actually possible that the historical and the symbolic are not mutually exclusive.

There is an inherent flexibility in the use of the term 'history' which should also put us on our guard. As well as the considerable differences in both concept and practice between ancient and modern history-writing, we should recognise a distinction between (a) a *historical* understanding of the Bible and (b) the understanding of the Bible *as history*.

It is inevitable that modern readers should acknowledge the Bible as essentially an antiquarian document, something which is given by history. It is therefore proper to write a history of the Bible as a collection of ancient documents. The authorisation of the text, and the setting of its limits, the canon, is the climax of that history. What follows after that climax is a further stage in the history of the interpretation of those texts. But this historical understanding of the Bible is a subject of study in its own right. Multi-volume works have been written on this subject, such as the *Cambridge History of the Bible*. For our present purposes we should concentrate on the second topic, the understanding of the Bible as history, or more strictly the examination of those texts which lay claim (at least in ancient terms) to be written history.

The work by Robin Lane Fox (1991) has already been mentioned. The aim of his enquiry is to ascertain whether the Bible is history, that is, whether it is true in either of two basic senses: first, is it internally coherent (logically, materially, doctrinally) and, second, does it correspond to the historical facts? Given the difficulties, which have already been acknowledged, with 'facts' in ancient history, a measure of agnosticism is appropriate. But Lane Fox's is a frankly atheistic reading of the Bible by an ancient historian whose own vision of the truth is grounded in a rationalistic, post-Enlightenment view of the historian's craft. It is almost an eighteenth-century view with echoes of the manner of Edward Gibbon. His targets are the Christian Churches, literary critics of the modern kind, liberal readers with a modernist tendency, and fundamentalists of all sorts. Perhaps the bias in ideological presuppositions needs to be acknowledged on both sides?

The Bible, as we have seen, is not one book but a whole library of 'writings' (as the Greeks called them). It is a heterogeneous collection, a tangled jungle of works in poetry and prose, originally composed in three different languages, and brought together over more than a millennium. It follows that one cannot judge all the component writings equally directly as works of history: some may be primary sources, others with a strictly subordinate contribution to make. But, as already discussed in the introduction, it also follows that there is an important aspect of the historical understanding of the Bible which is an account (reconstructed and some of it highly conjectural) of how the two separate collections (Old and New Testaments) were assembled, arranged, and ultimately came together.

What of the correspondence of individual books of the Bible to the facts of history? It is somewhat surprising that Robin Lane Fox concedes the invention of history as a genre to that court historian whom he sees as providing the narrative of King David's reign in 2 Samuel and 1 Kings. This writer is said to have a good case for being the 'world's first historian', long before the Greek historians Herodotus and Thucydides. He may well have drawn on an earlier memoir, since he wrote in the reign of Solomon; thus he is very close to a primary source. Lane Fox, for whom the model historian is the Greek Thucydides, is not too grudging in his praise of this Hebrew historian. Ironically much Old Testament scholarship now questions his existence as an individual historian rather than a much later school of thought about David.

A great German historian of the 1920s, Eduard Meyer, referred to Luke as the one great historian between Polybius (the last of the classical Greek historians) and Eusebius (the first great ecclesiastical historian of Christianity). Is it possible to catch a glimpse of what it meant to be a historian in the first century CE, when Luke would have been writing, by the use of a few comparative examples from Greek and Latin, Jewish and Christian history?

The Hellenistic writer Lucian in the second century CE produced a tract *On Writing History* in which he declared: 'The one aim and goal of history is to be useful; and this can result only from its truth. The one task of the historian is to describe things exactly as they happened.' Lucian has learnt his lesson, and acquired his passion for truth, from the much earlier example of Thucydides, who aimed to write history not for passing entertainment but for permanent usefulness. The historian must aim at accuracy and usefulness, in order that, when situations recur (as it was believed they must, according to a cyclic theory of history), people have the example of the past to teach them how to act in the present. This is the realm of lofty ideals, but Lucian does not mislead his readers into thinking that all historians work this way. Instead he attacks his contemporaries who emphasise the agreeable at the expense of the useful – 'such are the majority of historians who serve the present moment, their own interest, and the profit they hope to get from history.'

It is not just a simple distinction between historians who write to please their readers (and make money), and historians who write for the sake of truth. Few historians from the ancient world are uninfluenced by some doctrine of history. As we have seen, both Thucydides and Lucian imply a cyclic view of history, according to which 'there is nothing new under the sun' and events recur according to some elliptical continuum. It is also possible to write history to promote a cause. Does this only become propaganda when events are written up to exemplify the message, or history is rewritten periodically to account for ideological change? The celebrated Roman historian Livy (59 BCE–17 CE) commended the nationalist cause in these terms:

> Whatever may come of my work, I shall at least have the joy of having played my part in perpetuating the memory of the finest people in the world; and if in the midst of so great a multitude of writers my fame remains in obscurity, I shall console myself with the glory and the greatness of those who shall eclipse my repute.

Livy also expressed the essentially moral purpose in writing (and in reading) history:

> This is the most wholesome and fruitful effect of the study of history: you have in front of you real examples of every kind of behaviour, real examples embodied in most conspicuous form; from these you can take, both for yourself and for the state, ideals at which to aim; you can learn also what to avoid because it is infamous either in its conception or in its issue.

Because Livy's primary concern is for these two causes (the moral and the national) he does not distinguish too nicely between history and legend in presenting his case.

Luke's work may also call to mind the Jewish and Old Testament traditions of writing history, which involve looking at the course of events from a particular religious standpoint. The God of Israel is dynamic and active in historical events, leading his chosen people and rescuing them from calamity. Such a tradition may go back to the court historian, appreciated by Robin Lane Fox for his chronicles of King David and the succession of King Solomon. It is certainly reflected in the long sweep of the history of Israel's judges and kings, appraised by the Deuteronomistic historians in accordance with the theological principles of the religious law encapsulated in the book of Deuteronomy. The tradition persisted in the Greek dress of the books of the Maccabees, right at the end of the Old Testament era and not very long before the time of Luke.

Josephus was a Jewish historian writing in the first century CE. His account of the Jewish War against Rome (66–70 CE) contains much eye-witness material. In his introduction he promises to be impartial, but it becomes clear that his work is written from the standpoint of a Jew trying to restore his standing and gain the sympathy of the Roman public. He minimises, reinterprets, or omits all that might offend Roman susceptibilities. As a Jew he is also affected by the models of history in the Hebrew Bible that we have just noted. The success of the Roman siege of Jerusalem is attributed to two factors: 'the power of God over unholy men' (that is, the dynamic activity of God to punish the Jewish rebels) and 'the fortune of the Romans' (the idea of benevolent fate, Fortuna, derived from Italian paganism). Josephus's other works, such as the *Antiquities of the Jews* have clearly apologetic motives. His aim is to demonstrate the antiquity of the Jewish faith and to try to prove the unique validity of Jewish conceptions of history.

An adequate comparison with Christian traditions of writing history would take us several centuries later than Luke, probably as far as Augustine of Hippo in the fifth century CE. It has been said that Luke's work (as illustrated by attempts at coordination such as Luke 3.1) 'antiquated the apologetically intentioned portrayals of Church history in the second century, even before they appeared', and 'drew the author of Acts intellectually closer to Eusebius' in the fourth century. For a long time Christian history and classical history had little in common, so that classical history remained a pagan preserve. Christians were concerned with a particular group of historical events associated with Jesus of Nazareth. New converts from paganism did not really know where the history of Jesus fitted in with the history of Greece and Rome they had learnt at school, although comparative frameworks of dates might have existed. The tradition of Christian Church history developed by Bishop Eusebius of Caesarea (c.260–339 CE) was quite a different order of activity.

Eusebius traced the history of the Church from the time of Christ to the Great Persecution at the start of the fourth century; the story concludes with the conversion of the Emperor Constantine. Theologically he wished to demonstrate the continuity of the pure doctrinal tradition of Christianity in its struggle against both persecutors and heretics. A further stage in this process is reached by Augustine in the next century. He was conscious of the need for a new kind of historical apologetic for Christianity, where Christians and pagans could meet together on common ground. So Augustine commissioned Orosius to write the 'Seven books of histories against the pagans'.

These comparisons with a range of examples of history-writing assist in establishing a clearer perspective. If the author of Luke/Acts was a historian, then he was a historian as the ancient world understood it. This means telling the story, of ancient or recent events, to illustrate a theme of great relevance to the writer's and readers' own day. It may be more like a historical novel, or the recent television genre of the documentary drama, in the extent to which it depends upon imaginative reconstructions. The ancient historian may put words into the mouth of an emperor or general, as part of his narrative, simply in order to emphasise an interpretation of events that is essentially the historian's own. Some of the characterisations by the Roman historian Tacitus of political figures in his story may sound to us like the caricatures from *Spitting Image*. But the comments he was able to make by these means were just as pointed and telling as is the best of television satire.

To say this is by no means to devalue the texts on which we rely for ancient history. It is simply to acknowledge the bias and presuppositions of ancient writers, and to make allowance for these in the modern historical reconstructions which use all kinds of ancient writings, in combination with archaeological evidence and sociological and other interpretative models. Ancient historians can teach us much about the perspective on those events with which they are concerned. Tacitus, for example, makes an important acknowledgement of the rise of Christianity when, writing in the reign of the Emperor Trajan, he describes how Christians were treated by the Emperor Nero after the fire of Rome some fifty years earlier. Again, he relates this persecution by Nero to the death of Christ some thirty years before. This gives an 'alternative' historical perspective on Christianity within the Roman world. No commentator at the actual date of Christ's crucifixion would have been in a position to envisage the momentous implications of that particular event.

The writing which we find in the Gospel of Luke and the Acts of the Apostles shows that the author was an ancient historian seeking to interpret these events, of the life of Jesus and of the beginnings of the Church, for his own day (towards the end of the first century). The opening of the Gospel shows how much importance he attached to the proper ordering of a sequence of events. In many ways too his work still seems to have pioneered the idea of a biography of Jesus, with intentions significantly different from those of Mark and Matthew. In other words, Luke's work often needs to be contrasted with other first-century Christian preaching about the meaning of what Jesus said and did. (See, however, the writing of Richard Burridge for an alternative view.) And, to the best of our available knowledge, Luke's writing of the Acts was the first example of Church history, however idealised his picture of those early years may be.

There are other kinds of writing to be found in Luke's two works, which show that the author was not only an ancient historian. He possessed a strong theological sense of the continuity of the events of Jesus and the Church with the story of God's salvation of Israel, as revealed in the Old Testament. He set out to reinforce this message (of the Church as the new Israel, for the benefit of the wider world) by making deliberate echoes of the Old Testament in the way he told his story.

Because Luke wrote to interest a wider readership, he also fashioned an account of the missionary journeys of St Paul, to rival the romantic style of travel writing in the Hellenistic world. (See the section on Luke–Acts in chapter 2, pp. 35–7.) There was a whole genre of Hellenistic novels, studied and described by specialists such as Graham Anderson and Tomas Hägg. They include *Chaereas and Callirhoe* by Chariton of Aphrodisias, *The Ephesian Tale* by Xenophon of Ephesus, and Longus's *Daphnis and Chloe*. Most of these (with the exception of the last) involve their characters in extensive travels; to plot these on the map of the Mediterranean Sea produces an effect very similar to that of old schoolroom charts of Paul's journeys.

If Luke is set in these more accurately reconstructed contexts, appropriate for his era of history-writing, we can see better the kind of writer he was, and acknowledge the importance of his achievements and their value for his own time and for posterity. Luke appears as historian and imaginative writer, evangelist and theologian. He used the literary structures and the historical conventions of his time to communicate with his audience. What he communicates is not simply the idea of an early Christian community whistling to keep up its spirits in difficult days. Rather it is the earliest example of Christians in dialogue with the world around them, aware of political strategies and economic realities, and seeking to find a means of coexistence, mutual understanding and tolerance.

Chapter 2

Narrative theology

It is appropriate to begin this chapter with a story. This example is a fable, politically motivated and applied, as told by Professor Gervase Fen in the course of Edmund Crispin's detective novel *Buried for Pleasure*. Once upon a time

> there lived in a forest three foxes, named Shadrach, Meshach and Abednego. Shadrach had a fine suit of clothes and was immensely proud of it. Meshach had a portable gramophone and some records of dance music, to which he was greatly addicted. Abednego had a hogshead of ale, replenished monthly, with which he fortified himself against the manifold horrors of existence. In this fashion they co-existed for a long period, troubling little about each other. But there came a day when Meshach, communing with his soul in the forest to the accompaniment of a tango, discovered for the first time the obscene pleasures of righteous indignation. And having discovered them, he went to Abednego and communicated them to him, saying: 'Shadrach has a fine suit of clothes, and we have not. It is not just or equitable that Shadrach should be thus privileged.' So they went together to Shadrach, overpowered him, and took his fine suit of clothes away from him. But as there was only one fine suit of clothes and they could not agree which of them was to wear it, they burned it. So then nobody had a fine suit of clothes.
>
> And a year or so passed, and Abednego, whose indignation was more righteous than ever, went to Shadrach and said: 'Meshach has a portable gramophone and a number of records of dance music, and we have not. It is not just or equitable that Meshach should be thus privileged.' So they went together to

Meshach, overpowered him, and took his portable gramophone and his records of dance music away from him. But as there was only one portable gramophone and they could not agree which of them was to use it, they threw it into a pond. So then nobody had a portable gramophone.

And a year or so passed, and Meshach went to Shadrach and said: 'Abednego has a hogshead of ale and we have not. It is not just or equitable that Abednego should be thus privileged.' So they went together to Abednego, overpowered him, and took his hogshead of ale from him. But as there was not enough to be shared between them, they poured it all into a river. So then nobody had anything, and they were all so angry with one another that they quarrelled, came to blows, and thus fell an easy prey to a number of cannibal foxes which descended on them from the East and tore them limb from limb.

(1948, p. 150)

This fable uses, perhaps rather incongruously, the Old Testament names of Daniel's three companions in Babylon. The Old Testament is very readily associated, in the minds of many, with the idea of 'story' – with myths and sagas, fables, legends and theological narratives. The whole point of the Old Testament seems to be expressed by relating how God acted through the history of Israel. The belief that the world itself is God's creation is conveyed in stories of just how things began. The essential connection between the creation of the world and the history of Israel is represented by sagas about father-figures of humanity and of the nation.

To speak of stories entails the idea of a narrator, a storyteller, and equally importantly the existence of readers, or more likely of an audience. For stories retain indications that they are told out loud – a characteristic of orality – even when they are shaped within a tradition and written down. The readers respond, perhaps the audience heckles as well as applauds. Stories are told to attract attention, to entertain, to involve people as participants, and to leave a message in the mind. You will have noticed that I have already used a number of terms for 'stories': myths, sagas, legends and narratives. It is possible to give these terms distinct definitions, even to set them on a sliding-scale of value. The variation in terminology often indicates a subjective reaction rather than a scientific analysis. This is certainly the case with the popular sense of 'myth' as something untrue. It is better, then, not to reveal one's prejudices, but to use these terms as largely interchangeable.

The eminent American literary critic Harold Bloom, interpreter of *The Book of J* (1991), wrote in this way about the stories of the Hebrew Bible:

> These stories remain so original that we cannot read them . . . we are still part of a tradition that has never been able to assimilate their originality, despite many efforts to do so. I am thinking of such weird tales as Yahweh making Adam by scooping up some wet clay and then breathing upon it, or Yahweh sitting upon the ground under the terebinths at Mamre, devouring roast calf, curd, milk and bread, and then being offended by the aged Sarah's sensible derision when he prophesies the birth of Isaac. But there are uncannier tales of Yahweh that J tells us, such as Yahweh's impish behaviour when he confounds the bold builders of the tower of Babel; Yahweh's murderous and unmotivated attack on Moses in Exodus [4.24f], when poor Moses has camped at night on the way down to Egypt; and the extraordinary story of Yahweh burying Moses, with his own hands, in an unmarked grave.
>
> But beyond contrast is his [J's] choice of starting with the hard Judean spring. No shrub, no grass, but there is that flow welling up from the ground, watering the earth's dust, a welling up that presumably is at Yahweh's will, or should we say *is* Yahweh's will. That welling up is the prelude to Adam, and J's oddly characteristic pun or assonance, his false etymology of Adam from *adamah* [ground], wittily plays for its coherence upon the impishness of the childlike Yahweh. Given some wet clay, he fashions an image, but the model alone would have been a fake, an idol, and not a fiction, except for the spirit blown into our nostrils. Adam is a fake until Yahweh's own breath makes Adam a living being. How many ironies are we to read in this vitalizing fiction?
>
> (1989, pp. 6, 11)

The 'tradition' of which Bloom writes is of course both Jewish and Christian; generations of audiences and readers have wanted to assimilate these stories. Bloom's argument is that their essential originality is ineradicable. But the tradition of centuries adapts and conflates, perhaps blending the stories of Greece with those of Israel, in the course of a Christian tradition all too often characterised by anti-Semitism. A modern literary example can illustrate the point more strikingly, because of the way it has inverted the historical situation of the anti-Semitic pogrom. In Dan Jacobson's novel *The God-Fearer* (1992), Kobus the bookbinder and member of the dominant 'God-fearing' majority is haunted by two children dressed in the clothes of the persecuted Christer minority.

> Many years before, in his youth, Kobus had once read a Yavanit legend about a man who was pursued by hideous, stinking creatures called the Eumenides, or the Furies. They were ghosts from his past, tormentors of his conscience. He constantly fled in terror from them and they as constantly followed him. Then there came a day when he stopped running, acknowledged to others their presence in his life, and confessed to the crime that had impelled the Furies to follow him. Once this confession was made, lo and behold, the creatures transformed themselves into his helpers, his understanders; their name was changed too, and they became the Friendly Ones. They actually helped him (if Kobus's recollection of the tale was correct) to start building a great new city, in which justice would reign.
>
> Kobus would have hesitated on all sorts of grounds to compare himself with one of the ancient heroes of Yavan. And he would have hesitated even longer to compare his diminutive visitants with the terrifying, journeying creatures of the legend. And yet . . . What he wondered was the source of the power such stories had over us, if not in the chance they gave us to recognise ourselves in them, however feeble we might be, and however remote our lives might be in time and circumstances from the figures in the legends?
>
> (1992, p. 27)

Jacobson's fictional example emphasises the persistent and powerful influence of stories upon readers and audiences across the transforming span of centuries. Is there a particular style to such stories, something essential to their construction, which guarantees that they will achieve such a dynamic and absorbing effect? It would seem not, at least according to the character of Jehoshaphat in Stefan Heym's novel *The King David Report* (1973). (This is an East German novel which applies an Old Testament narrative to the political realities of Eastern Europe before the Berlin Wall came down.)

> Jehoshaphat ben Ahilud, the recorder . . . said that the members [of the Commission] had doubtless read, or had heard read, a great many books on a great many subjects and knew that there were various ways of telling a story: forwards or backwards, or starting in the middle and working in either direction, or mixing up everything, which was called tohubohu [chaos] and was quite the fashion among the more modern authors. However, he went on to say, for the purpose of the *Report on the Amazing Rise* and so forth, he felt that it was best to begin at the beginning, that is, with the anointment of young David by Samuel the prophet and with the Goliath story. Were the members agreed? The members did not object.

However readily associated the Old Testament may be with the idea of 'story', and of narrative as an effective means of targeting a message, it remains true that by the end of the twentieth century CE the residual memory of the actual content of Old Testament stories is meagre indeed. Imagine trying to retell at this moment, without any research, the stories to which Bloom and Heym refer! Many people would find that an impossible challenge, for the same reasons that questions on the Old Testament or classical mythology are least well answered in general-knowledge quiz programmes. Presumably this is also the explanation of the marked preference for retelling Old Testament stories in modern fiction. They are a rich resource that today is comparatively unfamiliar and under-explored in its detail. A provocative retelling of a multi-layered narrative can exploit the traditional understanding without offending many religious susceptibilities.

Among successful examples in modern fiction are the accounts of Noah's ark in Julian Barnes's story 'The Stowaway' (chapter 1 of *A History of the World in 10½ Chapters*, 1989) and in the short story by Gesualdo Bufalino entitled 'After the Flood *or* The Rude Awakening' (*The Keeper of the Ruins*, 1994, first published in Italian in 1986); the story of King David is also exploited in Joseph Heller's novel *God Knows* (1984) and one brief episode from 2 Samuel 13 in Dan Jacobson's *The Rape of Tamar* (1973). By comparison the New Testament seems under-used: I can think of no comparable instances in modern fiction of a fresh and critical retelling of a New Testament narrative. Perhaps blasphemy laws have protected Christianity from such attempts, while Islam was not saved from Salman Rushdie. But since this volume is concerned explicitly with reading the New Testament, mention should be made of a few older examples of a popular kind.

Lloyd C. Douglas was an American Lutheran clergyman, best known for his biblical novel *The Robe*, published in 1942. The story centres on the centurion who was involved in Christ's crucifixion and who subsequently tries on the purple cloak that Jesus had worn and becomes a Christian convert. But the novel is not simply the romantic treatment in the style of a biblical epic which this synopsis might suggest. Douglas had noted some of the progressive ideas among biblical scholars of his day, for example about the feeding miracle of the loaves and fishes.

It might seem strange that five thousand people would go out to hear Jesus, the wandering prophet, climb a mountain to sit at his feet, and yet not make any provision for what they would eat that day. The commentators suggested that most people had in fact brought food, although not everybody was so prudent. When Jesus saw those people who were hungry and in need, he made an extravagant gesture of generosity and hospitality, giving away everything which he and his disciples had brought with them. This example of sharing everything with others, so that nobody would go without, had a contagious effect. There was a general sharing, so everyone had plenty to eat, and indeed there were twelve baskets left over.

But even with incidents such as this, where scholarly interpretations might be offered within the telling of the story, the general impression made by *The Robe*, by Douglas's other novel, about Peter, *The Big Fisherman*, or for that matter by Henryk Sienkiewicz's *Quo Vadis* (1895) or Lewis Wallace's *Ben Hur* (1880) is that of a highly romanticised view of Christian origins. Such impressions, perpetuated as they have been by Hollywood film-makers, have little contact with historical research and biblical exegesis, or with the theological interpretation of narrative which is our present concern.

NEW TESTAMENT EXAMPLES FOR MODERN NARRATIVE THEOLOGY

In the absence of any suitable examples from the world of modern literature where the New Testament is used creatively, as we have seen the Old Testament has been, it may be necessary to make our own. Once again New Testament interpreters can follow the trail blazed by workers in the Old Testament. The opportunity is there, both for modern fiction and for biblical scholarship. A scholarly society, the Catholic Biblical Association, has even set up what they call a 'Task Force for the Study of Narrative in the New Testament'. One early result is a commentary on the Gospel of Matthew, *The Method and Message of Matthew* by Augustine Stock OSB (1994). The text of the Gospel is divided into three narrative parts:

1.1–4.16	The figure of Jesus Messiah
4.17–16.20	The ministry of Jesus Messiah to Israel and Israel's repudiation of Jesus
16.21–28.20	The journey of Jesus Messiah to Jerusalem and his suffering, death and resurrection

At first sight this does not seem to offer the most convincing case for the value of narrative theology, simply because Matthew's work is not really, or not merely, a narrative, but rather a teaching manual with narrative sections within it.

Here are three areas of New Testament text – both large and small – which can help to illustrate the methods used in narrative theology. These are, firstly, the implicit story which might be reconstructed between the lines of the correspondence in Paul's letter to Philemon; secondly, the broad sweep of narrative, the story that is told about the beginnings of Christianity in the Acts of the Apostles; and finally, the explicit, brief and self-contained story of the Walk to Emmaus in Luke 24.13–35.

Implicit and explicit narrative

It is obviously sensible for the study of 'theology in narrative' to concentrate on New Testament texts where the story is set out in the text and the theology can be teased out from the way the story is told. But just for the moment, and to make an informative contrast, let us examine instances where the theology stands in the text and the storyline has to be reconstructed hypothetically around it.

Probably the most difficult case is posed by the letters of John, particularly 2 and 3 John. Is it right to assume that the very brief letters, 2 and 3 John, are correctly embraced (as found in the New Testament) by the larger group of Johannine writings, from the Gospel to Revelation? Do they thus belong to an argument, or series of arguments, within the community, or against the community, about the theology of John? The task is to create a story featuring characters known as 'the Elder', 'the Lady', Gaius, Diotrephes and Demetrius. One must also decide whether it is Diotrephes or the Elder (John?) who is the heretic from the viewpoint of the mainstream Christian Church. That the problem can be stated in this way immediately reveals the meagre nature of the evidence for this historical story; we have to make some assumptions for any progress to be achieved.

Some reconstructions of the stories underlying the New Testament are almost entirely fictional. This does not deny them all legitimacy; it may be an excellent means of drawing out important theological implications, allowing themes to be seen in a new light. A case in point is the imaginative tour-de-force in the novella by Naomi Mitchison about Onesimus and Philemon, entitled *The Triumph of Faith*, to be found in the collection of her stories *When the Bough Breaks*. This extract sets the scene:

> I am Balas . . . a Cappadocian, never less than a faithful follower and soldier of the Unconquered Mithras. . . . I am steward to Menarchus, who owns half the valley, and has a great house in Colossae too; he trusts me and I am proud of it. His land marches with Philemon's from the river to the hill; but our side of the stone is the better ground, and, for all I say it myself, the better tilled as well. Philemon is an old man and bad at affairs, so he is in debt to my master. Five years ago things were going well with him; but his steward Onesimus, who was always a good friend of mine, ran away, taking with him all he could lay hands on in gold and silver. Menarchus need never be afraid of that with me. But Onesimus was a slave: and a Greek: and Archippus was often hard on him.
>
> (1974, pp. 53–4)

1. THE LETTER TO PHILEMON AND THE STORY OF ONESIMUS

Twenty-five verses of the New Testament provide all the information that is known from which the story of Onesimus might be reconstructed. It is natural to try and make this story explicit, for, as Norman Petersen remarked, 'if we as readers were asked to tell someone what the letter to Philemon is about, we would invariably respond by telling a story' (1985, p. 2). But which story should it be?

If the name 'Philemon' were all the evidence available, one might recall the story from Greek mythology about the generous and hospitable elderly couple, Philemon and Baucis. Theirs is a story of the Flood, and Philemon is the counterpart of Noah. Zeus and Hermes, disguised as needy travellers, tested humankind to see if any were worth preserving from the flood. All doors were closed to them, apart from a peasant cottage on a Phrygian mountainside, where the elderly couple did their best to welcome the strangers. The meal was frugal but prepared with devotion. Miraculously the flagon of wine kept refilling itself. The guests would not let Philemon and Baucis kill the only goose in their honour; they revealed their identity and showed the couple how the surrounding area had already been flooded. Only the cottage remained, now transformed into a marble temple, where the couple would serve the gods and die together, to be turned on their deaths into oak and lime trees.

The moral of the story might be the humanism expressed in these words, spoken by Zeus the traveller, in Nathaniel Hawthorne's 1851 version:

'When men do not feel towards the humblest stranger as if he were a brother,' said the traveller, in tones so deep that they sounded like those of an organ, 'they are unworthy to exist on earth, which was created as the abode of a great human brotherhood!'

J.B. Lightfoot, in his commentary on Colossians and Philemon (1880), made an observation only slightly less general:

The legend of Philemon and Baucis, the aged peasants who entertained not angels but gods unawares, and were rewarded by their divine guests for their homely hospitality and their conjugal love [Ovid, *Met.*, 7.626ff], is one of the most attractive in Greek mythology, and contrasts favourably with many a revolting tale in which the powers of Olympus are represented as visiting this lower earth. It has a special interest too for the Apostolic history, because it suggests an explanation of the scene at Lystra, when the barbarians would have sacrificed to the Apostles, imagining that the same two gods, Zeus and Hermes, had once again deigned to visit, in the likeness of men, those regions [Phrygia] which they had graced of old by their presence [Acts 14.11].

Jonathan Swift's 1709 version of this legend transposes the geographical setting to Kent and applies the moral to Christian hospitality:

> The Saints would often leave their Cells
> And strole about, but hide their Quality,
> To try good People's Hospitality . . .
>   for that Pack of churlish Boors,
> Not fit to live on Christian Ground,
> They and their Houses shall be drown'd;
> Whilst you shall see your Cottage rise,
> And grow a Church before your Eyes.

There is little even in the Christian version of this story, beyond the general ideal of brotherhood and the hope of generosity and service, to establish any connection with Paul's letter. It may then be only a coincidence of name. Although we might keep an original classical association in mind, we cannot rely on the name 'Philemon' alone to trigger the story, but we must look instead to the detail of the text.

Paul's letter follows a standard pattern which he adapted from the way such letters were written in the ancient world. First comes a formal greeting (verses 1–3), followed by an expression of thanksgiving (4–7). Then, it would seem, Paul presents his petition to Philemon on behalf of the runaway slave, Onesimus, asking that he would receive him back as a Christian brother. Paul respects Philemon's property rights as slave-master, and so he sends Onesimus back to his owner, with this as a covering letter, aiming to ensure, by all the means at his disposal, a favourable reception for the slave (8–21). Paul also drops a heavy hint that Onesimus has been of great value to him personally during his imprisonment; perhaps he hopes that Philemon will permit him to return to Paul.

What we do not know, of course, is how the story will end. Did Philemon respond well? Did he even take the hint, so that Onesimus could become one of Paul's co-workers? The fact that the letter is preserved at all within the pages of the New Testament might indicate that the response was favourable. The Church Father Ignatius, writing to the Ephesian Church (*Eph*. 1.3), indicates that he knows a bishop of Ephesus called Onesimus, who just might be the same person.

What can we say is the theology of this implicit narrative? An important issue is clearly the ethical question: how should the early

Christians react to the social fact of slavery? An American, J.H. Hopkins, writing in 1864 during the US Civil War, made a defence of slavery on the basis of the letter to Philemon:

> [Paul] finds a fugitive slave, and converts him to the Gospel, and then sends him back again to his old home with a letter of kind recommendation. Why does Paul act thus? Why does he not counsel the fugitive to claim his right to freedom, and defend that right? The answer is very plain. St. Paul was inspired, and knew the will of the Lord Jesus Christ, and was only intent on obeying it.

It is not really this simple, as can be seen by comparing the treatment of master–slave relations in Philemon with the ethical pattern set out in Colossians 3.22–4.1; Ephesians 6.5–9; and 1 Timothy 6.1–2. The formal codes of household relationships, included in these later letters, are concerned with the normality of social structures; they do not anticipate particular conflicts. By contrast, in writing to Philemon Paul has perceived a conflict represented by the social inequality of a master and his slave in this same Church. The details of the Onesimus story focus attention on this conflict. The fact that Paul wrote shows how important and dangerous he felt it to be.

To deal with the issue, Paul employs the ethical principle of 'love' as the norm of Christian conduct (verse 9, also 5,7). It is true that Paul is not attacking the existence of slavery as an institution of society; but he is attacking the problems which result from participation in the institution of slavery by a believing master and a believing slave. Christian love should mean that Onesimus is 'no longer a slave' but 'a beloved brother' (16). If the theme is restated in terms of obligation, then the outcome of the story means that Onesimus's indebtedness has been wiped clean by the fact of his return and by Paul's promise to pay the debt (18–19). But now Paul is calling in Philemon's debt which he owes to Paul himself (19).

But is even this story, so far, the correct way to interpret the evidence and draw out the implicit narrative and its theological implications? John Knox gave a modified account of the incident in his book *Philemon among the Letters of Paul* (1959). According to this, the actual master of Onesimus was Archippus, not Philemon, which explains why Archippus is mentioned in verse 2 as a recipient of the letter. Knox reckoned that the letter to Philemon was identical with that referred to in Colossians 4.16 as 'my letter to Laodicea' (Revised English Bible). So, in this version of events, Philemon is a prominent member of the Church in Laodicea (a neighbouring town to Colossae). Paul wrote to Philemon, so as to urge him to use his influence with Archippus on behalf of the latter's runaway slave, Onesimus. Philemon was expected to endorse Paul's view, either to Archippus in person, or more likely by sending the letter on to Colossae.

What difference does this juggling of the characters make to the real significance, the theology of the narrative? More than you might expect: not only does this account link Paul's letters together in a tighter network, but also the Christian Churches – and not just individuals – are seen to have a role in the story. Colossians 4.17 contains Paul's message to Archippus: 'See that you carry out fully the duty entrusted to you in the Lord's service' (Revised English Bible). The Greek word translated variously as 'task', 'duty' and 'service' is *diakonia*, a term to be used widely of specific ministries of the Church. Here Knox thinks it has a special content in relation to Archippus's reception of his slave.

Paul's letter to Philemon begins by addressing in the plural a group of people who are likely to have been leaders in the religious communities, including the house-church that is also mentioned. Norman Petersen describes the important leadership role of the host, 'the owner of the house in which the Church congregated'.

> To appreciate the role of host we need to remember that after the founding of a Church by nonresident missionaries like Paul and his fellow workers, these outsiders moved on to other cities and left the local Churches pretty much on their own, except for inspection visits by fellow workers, letters from Paul, or even visits by him if the situation demanded them.
>
> (1985, p. 297)

Although the letter then proceeds to address Philemon in the singular, it becomes clear that the issues in 'the Onesimus affair' concern the whole Church, or group of Churches. When local communities see themselves as essentially part of a larger movement of the Christian Church, what affects one may damage all. And so the pastoral influence from one community (such as Laodicea) can be brought to bear on a neighbouring Church (at Colossae). This is not the moment to regard another Church's concern as outside interference.

John Knox's reading of the Philemon letter represents a significant modification of the narrative; it is no longer just a personal story, but one which can affect the Church indirectly. But there is also another, quite different, narrative which can be reconstructed from the verses of the letter. This alternative story has been told by Sara C. Winter (1987, pp. 1–15). In her scenario the Church is involved directly, rather than by association. For the letter to Philemon is not a personal letter; Paul writes to a Church congregation, of which the named individuals are members or the leader. Onesimus the slave has been with Paul, not because he ran away from his master and by a (rather implausible) stroke of good fortune found someone with whom he could obtain sanctuary; no, he was actually sent to be with Paul by Archippus on behalf of the Church at Colossae.

Onesimus came from Colossae (Colossians 4.9). The Church had arranged for him to be with Paul as a visitor, to look after his needs during his period of house-arrest. A similar arrangement was made by the Church at Philippi in sending Epaphroditus to Paul (Philippians 2.25). When he writes to the Philippians, Paul is arranging to send Epaphroditus back to them for his sake, because he has been ill and is missing them so much. The case with Onesimus is similar, but different. The recipients of Paul's letter to Philemon know where Onesimus is, and that he is caring for Paul. If things had been otherwise, if Onesimus was an untraced runaway slave, then Paul was likely to have mentioned the fact in the 'thanksgiving' paragraph (verses 4–7) in which he sets the scene for the letter. But Paul is not even sending Onesimus back with his letter. On the contrary, Paul requests that Onesimus be released from his obligations in Colossae, so that he will not be required to return, but might remain with Paul, to continue his work in the Christian ministry.

Winter claims that no explicit mention is made in Paul's letter of Onesimus's actual return. What has misled readers in the past is an expression in verse 12, often translated 'send back', which can be used as a legal term for referring a case to the proper higher authority. One begins to realise how much the letter resembles a public document expressed in formal, legal language. So Paul is asking formally that his request for Onesimus's continued assistance should be considered with favour at the highest level in the Church at Colossae. In verse 17 'welcome' is then used in its figurative rather than in a literal sense (physical welcome): 'be favourable to his and my request.' The background to Paul's thought is expressed in verses 13, 14:

> All the time I intended to keep him in my service, in order that he might minister as your representative during my imprisonment for the Gospel; but I did not wish to do anything without your consent, in order that your good deed might not be by compulsion but voluntary.

The last part of Paul's request is concerned with the way the Church thinks of Onesimus. Paul asks that he should no longer be considered as a slave within the Christian community. In addition Paul intends to make a formal application for the manumission of Onesimus, and Paul is prepared to buy his freedom. Perhaps when the Church sent him to Paul he was simply a trusty slave owned by Archippus, sent to do what the Church leaders had ordered. But now, through his contact with Paul, he has become converted to Christianity, and so is infinitely more useful to the Christian mission.

There is more significance in the pun on the slave's name (verse 11) than is usually realised. Onesimus ('useful') was a fairly conventional slave's name, but the word-play – *achrestos* ('not-useful', i.e.'useless'), *euchrestos* ('very useful') – in its common element is only one letter different, and almost indistinguishable in sound, from the name of the Christ and thus of the Christian (*chrestos/christos*). The Roman author Suetonius, in his *Life of Claudius* 25.4, confuses these two words (but more likely from ignorance than as a deliberate pun); he refers to the emperor's decision to expel the Jews from Rome *c*.49 CE 'since they constantly made disturbances, at the instigation of Chrestus'. Christian preaching which stirred up the Jews is rendered by popular gossip as all the fault of some slave/agitator of the time. In the same way, Onesimus's conversion to Christianity makes him more than just a useful (but non-Christian) slave.

What, finally, is the theology of this alternative narrative? There seem to be two issues of particular significance. The first concerns the theme of ownership and the implications of Onesimus's conversion. This whole letter – in whatever way it is read – has been preoccupied with social relationships and stratifications. According to Norman Petersen's summary and caricature:

> Once upon a time there was a slave called Onesimus who became a brother to his master and a servant to his father, who

was also his brother (as well as a prisoner and ambassador or old man). Onesimus's father, Paul, on the other hand, was both a free man who was nevertheless a slave to a master, Jesus, who had himself been a slave, and a father to and partner with his child Onesimus's master, Philemon, who, like Onesimus, was also Paul's brother.

(1985, p. 2)

How should one deal with the complexity of relationships of superiority/inferiority within the Christian Church? Sara Winter's reading draws attention to the rhetorical use of five pairs of oppositions in verses 15 and 16. The effect is to progress through three levels of 'ownership': to own a slave, to own a Christian brother, to be owned by the Lord. Verse 16 states as an absolute fact that Onesimus as a Christian brother is 'no longer a slave' in the eyes of fellow-Christians. Ultimately all ownership is God's alone. What happened to Onesimus was through God's authority.

The second theme concerns the direct responsibility of the Churches. It encourages the reader to make a closer comparison between the reported activities of the Church communities at Colossae and at Philippi during the period/s of Paul's house-arrest. The letter to the Philippians strongly suggests the closest of supportive relationships between the Church and its apostle in a time of extreme hardship when his life was threatened. Paul, who did not normally claim the hospitality and subsidy which any teacher would have a right to expect, but valued his independence and worked to support himself, seems to have made an exception in the case of this Church (Philippians 4.15–16; compare 2 Corinthians 11.7–9).

The outcome was practical support when he needed it most, in prison and facing the death penalty. Even in such conditions the characteristic note of the Philippian letter (at least when taken at face value and not as ironic provocation) is overflowing joy and gratitude. If the letter to Philemon reveals a similar degree of practical assistance from Colossae at this or another time of Paul's need, then Philippi is not the unique case and Paul was more dependent than he usually cared to admit. The basis is a partnership and mutual support between co-workers ('fellow-soldiers' and benefactors); what Philippians expresses as the mutual 'satisfying' of needs (Philippians 4.18–19), can be conveyed in Philemon by the parallel metaphor of 'refreshment' (Philemon 7, 20).

In both cases economic realism in the face of need is close to the heart of Christian ministry.

The investigation of narrative theology now moves from the implicit, and conjecturally reconstructed, to the explicit story and theology. But even this is not straightforward, as will be seen. Part of the problem lies in the presuppositions about the texts that are used.

2. THE ACTS OF THE APOSTLES

Stephen Mitchell sounded such a warning when he observed in the *Guardian*, 30 April 1994, that 'we move from history to story in the way we use texts. Attempts to strip out a historical backbone from religious texts leaves them gutted.'

Nowhere is this attempt to isolate the historical fact more often made, and nowhere does it fail more frequently, than in the Acts of the Apostles. The moral seems to be that the broad sweep of the narrative has a historical characteristic, but that is far from claiming the details for history (in any modern scientific sense). Some of the problems of historical detail, and the concepts involved in writing 'history' in the ancient (classical) world, were discussed in chapter 1.

It would be possible to identify the fundamental 'story' of Acts, or of the Gospel of Luke and the Acts of the Apostles together, as a travel narrative, that is, as an account of a purposive journey. (The genre of travel writing in ancient literature is closer to the adventure novel than to the psychological self-exploration which is so regular a feature of the modern genre.) The 'journey' motif in Luke's writing, anticipated in the birth stories of Luke 1–2, is clearly seen in the progress of Jesus towards Jerusalem, which begins at Luke 9.51:

When the days drew near for him [Jesus] to be taken up, he set his face to go to Jerusalem.

The next ten chapters are principally concerned with the content of Jesus' teaching, but this is set in the narrative framework of a journey, which is clearly a literary device to heighten the tension dramatically. That it is an artificial construction is apparent if one tries to plot the journey on a map. Jesus leaves Galilee by the shorter route through Samaria, but reaches Jerusalem by the longer route through Jericho; meanwhile he is at Bethany, near Jerusalem, then on the borders of Galilee and Samaria.

The story of the journey has its theological importance in building up to what must happen in Jerusalem, to the necessity of Christ's suffering. Luke indicates the theological meaning at the outset by the unusual and evocative expressions he uses. Earlier in chapter 9 Luke has described a visionary experience, where Moses and Elijah appear with Jesus on the mountain.

> They appeared in glory and were speaking of his departure, which he was about to accomplish at Jerusalem.
>
> (9.31)

The word Luke uses for Christ's death, 'his departure' (*exodos*) is chosen deliberately because of its associations with a God-given event of deliverance, the Exodus of Israel from Egypt. Jesus' dying will be an even greater act of liberation. Similarly, at 9.51, Luke spoke of Jesus' being 'taken up' – his assumption or reception into heaven (*analempsis*). Not only does this point forward to the event at Luke 24.51 (and Acts 1.9), but also it recalls the story of Elijah's ascension (see 2 Kings 2.9–11). The figure of Elijah is prominent throughout Luke's depiction of Christ's prophetic work.

Just as Luke's Gospel refers to Jesus' journey, so correspondingly the Acts of the Apostles represents the advance of the early Church as a journey. This is projected in the structured summary of development in Acts 1.8:

> You will receive power when the Holy Spirit has come upon you; and you will be my witnesses in Jerusalem, in all Judea and Samaria, and to the ends of the earth.

Essentially this verse is a summary of the contents of Acts. The journey starts from Jerusalem, which is the strong link with Luke's Gospel, the scene of the death of Jesus, his appearances to the disciples after his resurrection, and his ascension. In Jerusalem the disciples are to receive the promised gift of the Spirit, and the city remains the setting for the first 7 chapters of Acts.

Acts 8.1 refers to a persecution which disperses the Jerusalem Church. For example, Philip goes to a city of Samaria (8.5). Clearly Judaea and Samaria become the settings for the next two chapters of Acts. The third and final phase will reach 'to the ends of the earth', as Acts 10–28 take the reader step by step, via the journeys of Peter and Paul, from Caesarea to Rome. The centre of the civilised world around the Mediterranean Sea, Rome itself is the fitting goal for the Acts of the Apostles. We should not think of the relatively quiet ending as an anti-climax. Rather it is a triumphant conclusion as the final objective is achieved by means of Paul's missionary journeys and his eventual arrest; through storm and shipwreck he arrives at Rome, where he preaches and teaches 'quite openly and unhindered' (Acts 28.31).

Other themes which interpreters of Luke/Acts have identified, such as justice and mercy, riches and poverty, women and men, prayer and the will of God, can all be seen in the light of this overall motif of 'the journey'. Consider, for example, the function of Christian initiation or baptism within the structure of Luke's narrative. Baptism is associated in a rather inexact way with the gift of the Spirit. This can be illustrated by the curious episode in Acts 8.4–25 which might be called 'the case of the incomplete baptism'. Why was it necessary to call in the people from headquarters? But the structural importance to the whole narrative of Acts is shown by the way the references to baptism and/or the laying on of hands are used as markers of the successive stages in the outreach of the Christian mission. This applies equally to the ministry of Peter and to the travels of Paul.

Luke never uses a story of a baptism taking place more than once in any one place. The effect of this scheme is that, each time a baptism takes place, the reader is alerted to the fact that the Christian mission has taken a new move outwards. The narrative gathers increasing momentum as with each story one observes that the settings move further and further from Jerusalem and Jewish culture, and nearer and nearer to the centre of the Roman empire. Acts is travel writing with a breathless purpose, and baptism is used as a kind of signpost pointing to the route. One might ask why there seems to be no baptism mentioned in Rome. It is just possible that there is a coded reference in the word 'unhindered' in the final verse, Acts 28.31. This word is often used in a technical sense in baptism accounts, such as 'What is to prevent me?' in Acts 8.36.

The special insights, and the working methods, of narrative theology can perhaps be demonstrated most clearly of all within the framework of one short story, that of the walk to Emmaus. This may be because the story acts as a microcosm of the Gospel in its potential effect on the reader; and possibly the original writer intended it to be so.

3. THE WALK TO EMMAUS (LUKE 24.13–35)

The overall point of this narrative is to be found both within the story itself (at 24.31: 'then their eyes were opened, and they recognized him') and also in the larger context of this chapter's presentation of Jesus' resurrection and the incredulity about reports of his appearances (e.g. 24.11: 'the story appeared to them to be nonsense, and they would not believe them'). The issue is one of 'true epistemology' – the authentic way of recognising Jesus and believing in the fact of his resurrection.

The narrative works its way to this climax by means of three structured oppositions as identified and described by Daniel Patte.

1 Jesus asks the walkers (24.17) about the subject of their animated discussion; but they cannot believe that anyone in Jerusalem is unaware of the news. Cleopas's words (24.18) imply a strong rebuke. The walkers assume that they know what has happened and find Jesus guilty in apparently not knowing. Theirs is a false confidence. In fact, Jesus, not they themselves, possesses complete knowledge.

2 The disciples explain what happened and their reactions (24.19–24). At this Jesus rebukes them (24.25–7): 'How dull you are! How slow to believe!' What the disciples lack is the key to interpret the situation, namely an understanding faith in the scriptural prophecies. But even when Jesus explains, it does not seem that the disciples recognise what has happened and who Jesus is.

3 When the disciples arrive at their destination, Jesus 'made as if to continue his journey' (24.28b). But the disciples press Jesus to stay (24.29). The text of the story continues to operate from within the disciples' perceptions. They want to help the stranger, particularly because the hour is late. They offer hospitality and provide honour to their guest by allowing him to preside at their meal. The moment at which he blesses and breaks the bread is the moment of perception and long-delayed recognition. But it is the disciples' action in generous hospitality which has precipitated the symbolic action of their guest with the bread. This symbolic action obviously recalls previous occasions when Jesus had done this, and it seems to provide the Church with a model for future action.

Obviously there are other meals in Luke's Gospel – the logic of the present story requires that there should have been – but their significance only emerges in retrospect. As the readers of the

Gospel arrive at the climax to Luke's narrative, the story itself opens their eyes to the deeper meaning of past words and actions. It is also possible to argue that the story of the table fellowship between Jesus and his disciples at Emmaus represents the major point of transition between the meals before Jesus' death and the meals celebrated by early Christians. By this story the pattern is set of Christian worship as a combination of word and meal. The teaching from Scripture and the breaking of bread are essentially complementary, not exclusive alternatives.

A further aspect of this narrative is the indication which it gives of a potential to become interactive, to engage the reader with dramatic intensity, and to lift a story from the past into an inspiration for the present and the future (compare chapter 4, pp. 64–9). In Marjorie Reeves's words,

> And so, in the New Testament, the Master of Dialogue meets us. He meets us in those life-changing encounters with Nicodemus, with the Samaritan woman, with Zacchaeus, with Mary Magdalen, with the disciples on the Emmaus road. Those short sentences spoken in the scene with the woman taken in adultery take our breath away in their immensity. When Jesus utters that one potent word 'Mary' on Easter morning or again 'Peace be with you' on Easter evening, speech – our *human* speech – is carried up into transcendence. The words were presumably spoken in Aramaic, a particular language in time and space, but they have the ring of eternity. Immanence and transcendence meet.
>
> (1992, p. 4)

The same potential seems to be represented visually in Caravaggio's painting *The Supper*:

> At Emmaus the startled disciples pull back as Christ, blessing the bread, reveals himself to them. It is a moment captured in silence. We and the disciples are forcibly caught up in awe for the divine purpose.
>
> (*Church Times* on National Gallery exhibiting of Caravaggio's work, 24 February 1995)

CONCLUDING OBSERVATIONS

Most obviously in this method of reading, the narrative itself, which is the dominant concern, is the text in its final (canonical) form, viewed in a multi-faceted and holistic way. There could be no greater contrast than with the historical-critical method which seeks to excavate the original layer beneath the text as it stands, and often yields a fragmenting of the text.

As with other literary approaches, in a modern context of pluralism, there can be no guarantee that any one reading of the text is uniquely correct. Each reader may champion her/his own reading and its associated theology, while acknowledging that other readers and other situations may demand a different 'narrative'. Especially in the case of reconstructed (once implicit) narratives, there is a wide recognition of alternative stories which can be equally valid and meaningful. The major exception to such pluralism is the more fundamentalist position where the literary device of the narrator's omniscient point of view is held to correspond to God's omniscience and therefore to guarantee a particular conclusion as the 'point of it all'.

An interesting comparison can be found in an earlier age of literary theory. Franz Kafka put these quite radical remarks in his diary in 1911:

> In general a spoken sentence starts with its capital letter with the speaker, bends out as far as it can to the listeners and then returns with a full stop to the speaker. But if the full stop is omitted, then the sentence, no longer constrained, keeps flying right out to the listener at full length.

Obviously different conventions (e.g. punctuation) apply in other languages and cultures. But Kafka's remarks represent an intermediate position, where the author seeks to keep control of the outward structure, while involving the readership fully in the content of the communication.

When applied to the Gospels and the Acts of the Apostles, narrative theology can tend to be conservative in critical outlook, because of the concern for the unity of the text. There is much emphasis upon the artistry of the literary constructions of the authors. Someone who writes so powerfully must be trustworthy! To take this step shows a reader who is still hankering after identifications of the original author's intention, and the original setting and purpose of the text. But it is equally possible to read in a much more radical way, thus identifying (for instance) a feminist message from the text, which might be thought at odds with any original intention of a male author.

In many New Testament stories the principal characters are male. When there are female participants, as for example in Jesus' visit to the house of Mary and Martha (Luke 10.38–42) or the anointing of Jesus by the woman in Mark 14.3–9, the traditional reading of the stories, and presumably also the evangelist's original intention, is to focus on Jesus himself and on the women only in their relation to Jesus. To read or retell the story with a female emphasis has dramatically different consequences. It is not just a matter of reading the Gospel texts through women's eyes and observing that the historical Jesus directed his mission to the poor, sick and social outcasts of his day, and therefore to women as among the poorest and most neglected layers of society. But it may also mean, as Julie Hopkins writes, that

> It is only possible to bring women into the centre of an incarnational christology if the traditional categories are gender reversible; if, in other words, we may speak of the Divine incarnated in a female body, 'truly God and truly female' or as the Dutch feminist theologian Anne-Claire Mulder argues, we may speak of the female flesh becoming Word/Logos. If this proves to be impossible on Christian theological or moral grounds, then I must sadly conclude that Mary Daly was correct when she observed, 'If God is male then the male is God' and 'Salvation comes only through the male'.
>
> (1995, p. 85)

We have already noticed the interactive potential of a text within narrative theology. It challenges the involvement of the modern reader at a deep level. The point is well illustrated in the unpublished narrative commentary on Mark's Gospel by B. Van Iersel of Nijmegen, commenting on Mark 3.35:

> *For whoever does the will of God, that is my brother and sister and mother.* What is true of those about Jesus applies also to the readers of the book, then and now. The new family of Jesus is not a naturally closed group of relatives, nor is it limited to the characters in the story. It is, in fact, an open circle with room for many – that is to say, for all kindred spirits. These are not just characters in a story but also flesh and blood human beings outside the text, who whether or not as readers of the story respond to Jesus with faith.

The most obvious way to interpret the text is by retelling the story with an explicit heightening of the theme in the direction of the modern reader. But interpretations using another medium, such as poetry, drama, dance, liturgy or visual imagery, would be equally possible and valid. The point is not just to analyse the interpretation as for the original readers (this is to treat the text after the manner of an historical exhibit in a museum) but also to give it another dimension of relevance, as a direct expression which speaks to the situation of today's readers. It feels as if the Gospels have the ability to pull the audience into the story, so that criticism and encouragement of the disciples in the narrative is implicitly addressed to those who hear and read the story.

The newer processes of literary criticism have recognised how inevitable it is that the readers are the ones constructing meaning from the text. But should there be some ethic or aesthetic in the reading process, to function as a criterion or control over the manner or content of the retelling? To propose this might be seen as a rearguard action to campaign for the author's interests, or to protect the traditions of the Church and to argue for consistency between then and now. Yet if the act of reading is as much part of a process of inspiration, as the original writing was thought to have been, there might well be the need for controls or standards of discrimination, to judge which are the truly inspired voices for our situation.

Chapter 3

Short stories and their structure

The modern short story is a literary fascination. As Malcolm Bradbury writes in *The Penguin Book of Modern British Short Stories*:

> The short story has become one of the major forms of modern literary expression. . . . For what we usually mean by the genre is that concentrated form of writing that, breaking away from the classic short tale, became, as it were, the lyric poem of modern fictional prose. . . . The modern short story has therefore been distinguished by its break away from anecdote, tale telling and simple narrative, and for its linguistic and stylistic concentration, its imagistic methods, its symbolic potential. . . . In fact, for many prose-writers it has become closest to representing the most 'poetic' aspect of their craft.
>
> (1987, p. 11)

V.S. Pritchett, in his introduction to *The Oxford Book of Short Stories*, seems to agree:

> The short story springs from a spontaneously poetic, as distinct from a prosaic, impulse – yet it is not 'poetical' in the sense of a shuddering sensibility. Because the short story has to be succinct and has to suggest that things that have been 'left out', are in fact there all the time, the art calls for a mingling of the skills of the rapid reporter or traveller with an eye for incident and an ear for real speech, the instincts of the poet and ballad-maker, and the sonnet writer's concealed discipline of form. The writer has to cultivate the gift for aphorism and wit. A short story is always a disclosure, often an evocation – as in Lawrence or Faulkner – frequently the celebration of character at bursting point: it

approaches the mythical. Above all, more than the novelist who is sustained by his discursive manner, the writer of short stories has to catch our attention at once, not only by the novelty of his people and scene, but by the distinctiveness of his voice, and to hold us by the ingenuity of his design. . . . A modern story comes to an open end. People are left carrying the aftermath of their tale into a new day of which, alarmingly, they can as yet know nothing.

(1981, p. xiv)

Perhaps it was ever so. Even the shortest of short stories can grab the attention, present a riddle, or open a new dimension of thought, engaging the reason with a problem to be solved. So, for example, there are stories in the Jewish tradition, such as these two recalled by the novelist Chaim Potok:

An old Hasid called his sons together and told them that he wished them to divide his property in a certain way after he departed for the True World. The oldest son was to take one-half; the next son, one-third; the youngest son, one-ninth. Soon afterward the old Hasid was called by the Master of the Universe to his eternal rest. The sons wished to obey their father, but they discovered that their father's property consisted of seventeen goats, and seventeen cannot be divided by one half or one third or one ninth. They didn't want to kill any of the goats and divide it, because each goat was much more valuable alive than dead. And so they went to the Rebbe, and in his wisdom the Rebbe immediately solved their problem. What did the Rebbe tell them?

There was a Hasid who owned a little lamb, a big cat, and a big dog. It is known that big cats can do great harm to little lambs, and big dogs can do great harm even to big cats but will never hurt little lambs. The Hasid cared for his animals, was with them always, and prevented them from quarrelling and, God forbid, harming one another. Now it happened that one day there was a terrible storm, and the river rose outside the home of the Hasid and threatened his life and the lives of his animals. The Hasid had to get himself and his animals to the other side of the river, where there was a hill that would protect them from the rising water. But he had only one little boat, and in that boat he could only take with him one animal at a time. How did the Hasid get the animals across the river in such a way that they did not harm each other when they were left on the riverbanks without him?

(1992, p. 245)

The function of short stories, whether seen in such Jewish riddles, or in the literary craft of later generations, could be described in the words of Novalis (the eighteenth-century German poet and philosopher Friedrich Leopold von Hardenberg):

> By giving what is commonplace an exalted meaning
> what is ordinary a mysterious aspect
> what is familiar the impressiveness of the unfamiliar
> to the infinite an appearance of infinity.

Some of the most striking examples of this 'short-story phenomenon' can be seen in the parables attributed to Jesus in the Gospels. According to Sallie TeSelle, 'parables are metaphors, setting the familiar in an unfamiliar context, moving us to see our ordinary world in an extraordinary way' (1975, p. 4).

This point is made, as the subject within the story itself, in a Jewish parable, here quoted from Elie Wiesel's *A Beggar in Jerusalem*, but essentially a variation upon a traditional theme:

> One day a man leaves his home, his native village where time does not exist, and goes off in search of a rainbow, an adventure. He heads toward the faraway and magic city. Evening falls and he is caught in the midst of a forest. He selects a tree with thick foliage under which to spend the night, sheltered from wind and rain and thieves. Before falling asleep he removes his shoes and places them nearby, pointed in the direction of the road he is to follow in the morning. Could he foresee that around midnight, in order to confuse him, punish or save him, a practical joker would turn his shoes around, pointing them back toward his village?
>
> At dawn he arises, thanks God for giving back his sight and soul to him, and suspecting nothing, continues merrily on his way. From a hilltop, he sees at last the mysterious, promised city. He had imagined it larger, different. Seen from nearby, it seems curiously familiar: the river, the gardens, the crossroads are exactly like those in his hometown. Moreover, he thinks he can recognize each building and guess who lives there. To the right: the inn and its drunkards, dirty not because they like dirt, but

because they distrust water. Farther on: the city hall, with its faded tricolored flag hanging down from its pole like the head of a tired old horse. To the left: the police station, serving as buffer between the grocer and the butcher, at loggerheads more as a matter of tradition than of necessity. Behind the municipal theater: the market, where the visitor knows what each housewife will buy, at what cost, and from which farmer. Feeling more surprised than disappointed, our traveller thinks: 'Well now, they've told me lies. The big city has nothing to boast about, it holds no secrets, maybe it doesn't even exist, only my village exists, it is its image I see reflected in the world.'

From that moment on, nothing astonishes him. He knows that turning the next corner, past the shoemaker's, he will find himself in front of a house just like his own. Yes, the door is slightly ajar. 'Odd, the lock needs fixing, just like at home.' From inside, a voice invites him to enter: 'You must be hungry, come and eat.' He could swear it is his wife's bossy, whining voice. It is enough to drive him mad, but being hungry, he might just as well obey and not make a fuss. Besides, he has always obeyed his wife. He crosses the kitchen and enters the living room with its windows facing a court bordered with greenery. He sits down at the table. The children smile at him, and he is overwhelmed by sadness. The smallest one clutches at his knees, plays with his beard and whispers in his ear: 'You'll stay with us, won't you? You won't leave us, will you?' Because he does not want to disappoint the child and because he feels that it's no use, he is trapped, the stranger caresses the child's golden hair and ends up promising him everything.

He kept his promise. He never returned to his village. Death went looking for him there, but did not find him.

(1996)

We should look at some of the Gospel parables attributed to Jesus in more detail and try to analyse what is happening and how the story works. From a rich choice the parables of the sower and the prodigal son are selected as examples. In the first instance the original form of the sower parable might be reconstructed from a comparison of the versions in the Gospels of Mark, Matthew, Luke and Thomas. J.D. Crossan (1980) claimed to have found the 'ancestral text' in Thomas and a prototype of Mark:

Now the sower went out, took a handful [of seeds], and scattered them. Some fell on the road; the birds came and gathered them up. Others fell on rock, did not take root in the soil, and did not produce ears. And others fell on thorns; they choked the seed(s) and worms ate them. And others fell on good soil and produced good fruit: it bore sixty per measure and a hundred and twenty per measure.

(Gospel of Thomas 9)

A sower went out to sow. And as he sowed, some seed fell along the path, and the birds came and devoured it. Other seed fell on rocky ground, where it had not much soil, and immediately it sprang up, since it had no depth of soil; and when the sun rose it was scorched, and since it had no root it withered away. Other seed fell among thorns and the thorns grew up and choked it, and it yielded no grain. And other seeds fell into good soil and brought forth grain, growing up and increasing and yielding thirtyfold and sixtyfold and a hundredfold.

(Mark 4.3b–8)

There can be no certainty about original forms, but it is important to ask such questions and attempt a (speculative) reconstruction. This parable, according to Crossan, has five basic units: the act of sowing, the path, the rocks, the thorns, and the good soil.

According to Mark 4.11, the parable is related to 'the secret of the kingdom of God'. But it is not just teaching about the nature of God's kingdom; it is also teaching about the action of teaching about the kingdom. For our purposes, too, it is an excellent example, because it is a kind of 'metaparable' (an ultimate super-parable), as it is a parable about the parables of the kingdom. By paying special attention to the different constructions and emphases in Matthew's and Luke's version, it is possible to suggest how different evangelists, interpreting the 'ancestral' form of the parable, construed the action of teaching by parable in different ways. Frank Kermode, writing in *Genesis of Secrecy*, states the idea even more forcibly by calling the parable an allegory for the act of interpretation as such. (For the definition and discussion of allegory see chapter 8 below.) The interpreter is expected to be someone with privileged information, on the inside of the story; but the apparently authorised interpretations of the parable are so dubious that the interpreter is shown to be in reality an outsider in relation to the text.

Crossan says that the parable is not about the sower, but about the seed and the yield. The crop's eventual yield is a *plurality* of possible realisations, not only for the kingdom of God and its manner of arrival, but also for the interpretation of the parable as well. The parable of the sower prefigures the potential variety in its own readings and misreadings. In Crossan's words:

> When the tradition changed the parable internally in the transmission, or when Thomas omitted any explicit explanation, and the pre-Synoptic tradition added a canonical explanation, or when exegetes, ancient and modern, deliberate intention and multiply meaning, all that happens is that the polyvalence asserted for the yield is repeatedly verified.
>
> (1980, p. 51)

The parables in Mark's Gospel function both to reveal and to conceal ultimate truth. In this manner divine revelation is not something which is ultimately clarified once for all, but it becomes a vehicle for new revelations, dependent upon the motivation and inspiration to interpret the story anew. Parables ('similitudes') are used in a similar way in the early Christian work (just outside the canon of the New Testament) *The Shepherd of Hermas*.

Paul Ricoeur defined parable as 'the conjunction of a narrative form and a metaphorical process'. To these two features of metaphor and narrative form Crossan adds a third defining characteristic, that of brevity (or, we might say, radically sharp focus). If, with Ricoeur and Crossan, it is argued that metaphor is indeed the constitutive principle of language in general, then there is no such thing as language that is non-metaphorical, non-rhetorical. In Crossan's words, where the real issue lies is

> not in setting existence against language,
>   or world against metaphor,
>   or reality against narrative,
> but in facing the ultimate implications of a radically linguistic existence, a radically metaphorical world, and a radically narrative existence.
>
> (1980, p. 13)

Crossan reads Jesus as someone who did something very like that within his parable teaching. In contrast to Rabbinic parables within the later Jewish tradition, where the context leaves little doubt as to the meaning of the parables, Jesus' strategy was the direct opposite.

One must therefore add a fourth defining characteristic of parable: that of paradox. This is a deliberate and extravagant use of paradox. Crossan sees it as a late expression of, and reaction against, Israel's rejection (as in the Ten Commandments) of any image of the one God. This process seems to have generated the use of paradox in preference to a simple image, and produces single paradoxical images, double contradictory images, or multiple and polyvalent images of its God. By these means God is not trapped in the forms of language or the figures of art. Jesus' use of parables could then be said to anticipate the *via negativa* of theology (God is ineffable and human language is hopelessly inadequate). The poetic parable operates at the limits of language, evoking the other side of silence, ultimately ceasing to reveal anything of the character of divinity, but only its unknowability.

We should now turn to analyse the second example among the parables attributed to Jesus, the story of the prodigal son which is found uniquely in Luke 15.11–32. We can use this example to consider the questions of a parable's structure. On the level of a surface reading, it can readily be observed that the story has a complex plot. Although usually known by the title already used, and therefore orientated around the younger, and prodigal, son, the range of the story is more adequately covered by a title such as 'A Father Had Two Sons'. All three of the main characters could become the focus of the story, so it could equally well be known as the parable of the 'elder brother', or the story of the 'father's love'.

Two verses of a hymn written by Kevin Nichols (*Complete Celebration Hymnal*, 1984, no. 577) illustrate the last of these readings:

Our Father, we have wandered and hidden from your face,
in foolishness have squandered your legacy of grace.
But now, in exile dwelling, we rise with fear and shame,
as distant but compelling, we hear you call our name.

And now at length discerning the evil that we do,
behold us, Lord, returning with hope and trust to you.
In haste you come to meet us and home rejoicing bring.
In gladness there to greet us with calf and robe and ring.

This reading assumes that the parable is addressed, not (as is usually suggested, e.g. by Joachim Jeremias) to the scribes and Pharisees who criticised Jesus for familiarity with sinners, but to those sinners themselves. The prodigal son represents all sinners who have wandered from God's love. The father's gifts are initially squandered, but here the gift of God is summed up in terms of divine grace.

If we look more deeply at the structural grammar of this complex story (three stories in one), it would help to follow the sequence of expectation for each of the sons. As regards the younger son, his father's division of the property provides for the son's well-being. The son becomes the subject of the sequence, and he expects the share of the property, coupled with his own initiative and entrepreneurial skill to help him on his way. But the younger son becomes his own worst enemy, establishing, together with the famine and other hostile factors, a fundamental opposition to his plans. The only way remaining for the son, in order to ensure his well-being, is to take steps to enlist his father's help. The consequence of this is for the father again to become the subject of the story, displacing his son from control of his own affairs.

In the sequence that is the elder son's story, the objective is to achieve the acceptance back into the family of the younger son, despite all his prodigality. The father works to achieve this and to celebrate his son's return. The audience expects the elder brother to be the villain of the story, and he duly complains and seeks to oppose and frustrate his father's wishes. It is only at the end of the story, when the father refuses to accept his elder son's opposition and polarisation of the issue, that the audience realises that it has been told a different story from the expected one. The twist in the end of the story reveals a parable about two sons, where the father remains throughout the real subject of the action, and each of his sons opposes him in turn. The favourite younger son, the prodigal, is an opponent of his father's will. The elder son's opposition is really directed against his father's actions, not simply motivated by jealousy of his younger brother. To appreciate the paradox of the story, the audience has to abandon the plot it expects to hear. Only in that way can one experience with the father his tragic rejection by each son, and also appreciate his joy at retaining both of them.

The route we have been following, in describing the narrative sequences and structural grammar of this multi-faceted parable, is effectively offering a structural analysis without using too much structuralist jargon. It is important to notice that there is no single method or solution provided by structuralism. Instead there are several, as described by Mark Stibbe in his reading of John's Gospel in this series (1994). Most structuralism begins from the pioneering work of Ferdinand de Saussure in analysing the fundamental structures of language. The first approach derives from the work of Claude Lévi-Strauss (and subsequently Edmund Leach) in social anthropology and the analysis of myth. This is known as the *binary* approach, because it seeks to identify binary oppositions within biblical stories, and to assess how far these oppositions are mediated. A second approach derives from the investigation by the Russian Vladimir Propp of the finite number of variations in folktales (thirty-one possible functions of seven character types). This approach, called the *functional*, describes the functions or actions in the plot of a biblical story, and compares this story with others sharing the same deep structure.

The third approach, which is more recent and most often employed today by all who have not renounced structuralism, is a substantial adaptation of Propp's morphology by the French structuralist A.J. Greimas, which is also applied in the work of Roland Barthes. This is known as *actantial* analysis, and consists in charting a particular biblical story against a universal structure, a fundamental narrative grammar which all narratives are believed to obey. In this respect a narrative is nothing more than 'a long sentence', according to Barthes. Daniel Patte, the French-Canadian, one of the foremost biblical structuralists, has developed actantial analysis with considerable sophistication and complexity, regarding language as a cultural code (see his treatment of the Emmaus story, referred to in chapter 2). Greimas's type of analysis is frequently presented in terms of a diagram, an actantial model, which seeks to clarify the structure and certainly helps to accentuate the surprise factor in a particular version of a story. Greimas's view of the deep narrative structure, permanently underlying all narratives, is represented in Figure 3.1.

Figure 3.1 reveals six different poles of character within a narrative (subject, object, sender, receiver, helper and opponent). The deep structure has three axes representing basic functions of the plot within the story (communication, power and volition). The axis of communication is a commission: someone is telling someone else to do something. A story usually begins when a sender tells a receiver to undertake a task. The axis of volition represents the quest: the hero undertakes this particular task, to fulfil a mission. The power axis represents the conflict experienced in the quest, and the struggle to execute it. In this model are the

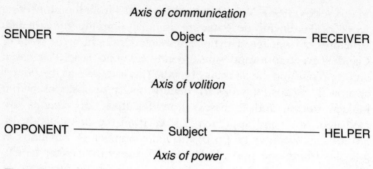

Figure 3.1

characters and functions of the plot which we have already seen illustrated in the story of the father with two sons. Figure 3.2 represents the story about the well-being of the younger son, which the audience is anticipating; whereas Figure 3.3 represents the story which the audience is told. The element of surprise for the audience must be reckoned as great as when the hated opponent of the Jews becomes the saviour of the Jewish victim (the Good Samaritan of Luke 10.30–35), or when the 'great tree' as the expected cosmic symbol of the coming kingdom turns out to be the plant grown from a mustard seed (Matthew 13.31f).

We have used these two examples of parables attributed to Jesus in order to investigate the workings of such short stories, and identify their literary, theological and structural characteristics. To conclude this chapter we should now attempt to summarise

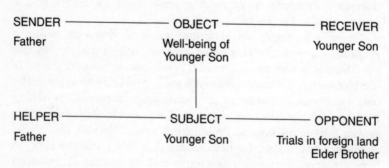

Figure 3.2

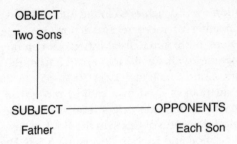

OBJECT
Two Sons

SUBJECT ——————— OPPONENTS
Father   Each Son

Figure 3.3

the essential features of such stories, recognising their origins in oral transmission, but focusing on their presentation in a literary context. Our concern is with story and plot, characters and setting, author's point of view and audience/reader response.

The literary critic Seymour Chatman made an influential distinction between *story* and *discourse* in his book of that title, published in 1978. Story indicates what a narrative is; discourse shows how a story is told and how it is made to work. Discourse relates to rhetoric in new literary criticism (and more detail on this can be found in the latter part of chapter 5). Discourse is where the author and the reader/audience interact with each other (or at least where the implied author and reader, both implied by the story, are expected to interact). Anyone – who is not the author – in reading a text in order to perceive its meaning must, by definition, be creating a receiver's perceived meaning. Any reader who is implied by the text is creating a receiver's perceived meaning, but of course that meaning is the one the author intended to convey at that point. All this activity of discourse happens in reality or in theory 'in front of' the text. But it is still legitimate for us to analyse the components of the story itself, which has provoked this reaction, even though the act of interpreting the components may effectively move them into the realm of discourse.

Characters are obviously essential to a story. Actions are carried out by participant characters, even if the story itself is a monologue by the narrator. Characters may be known by what they say or do, or by what is done to them or said about them. Narrative analysis of characters is inseparable from analysis of plot, simply because the plot of a story is made from the interaction of its characters. At the period when the New Testament documents were written, characterisation was not achieved in the full, rounded and romantic or realistic manner of more recent fiction. In ancient literature, characters were more often established as stereotypes or stock figures, sometimes with significant variation from the norm. In the parable of the Good Samaritan (Luke 10.30–35) the stock figure of the hated Samaritan is used in a radical reversal of expectation. Creativity in characterisation offers dramatic possibilities, as with the paradoxical depiction of Christ in the Book of Revelation by the juxtaposition of lion and lamb in Revelation 5.5–6. Here, of course, symbolism is exploited fully. Similarly there is dramatic contrast between the women of the Apocalypse, contrasting the mother of the Messiah in Revelation 12, the harlot Babylon in chapter 17, and the new Jerusalem as a bride in Revelation 21.

While characterisation answers the question 'Who?' about the story, the setting supplies the answers to 'Where?' and 'When?'. The work of Elizabeth Struthers Malbon, discussed in chapter 5 below, illustrates the importance of place as well as timing from a literary critic's – as opposed to a historian's – point of view. These discussions reflect the pace of the narrative and the symbolic associations of various localities as contexts of the action. Details of time and place are no longer the exclusive preserve of those seeking fragments of realistic evidence as part of a quest for the historical Jesus. The road from Jerusalem to Jericho, which is the setting of Luke's parable of the Good Samaritan, has a symbolic value that is more than the fact of the route one can travel today, passing the Inn of the Good Samaritan. To take another example from the Apocalypse, one can note the frequency of references to the heavenly throne of God – forty-seven occurrences in Revelation out of sixty-two in the whole New Testament. Such a dominant setting for the action of this book could be taken, as James L. Resseguie suggests, to symbolise

> God's rule which is directed outward, toward his creation, in contrast to human rule which is directed inward, towards itself. God's rule is life-sustaining and life-giving rule which accounts for the image at the end of the Apocalypse of 'the river of the water of life' flowing out of the throne.

(22.3)

Also in Revelation there is a dramatic contrast of place between the two cities, Babylon and Jerusalem. Babylon is the city of depravity which presents a devilish parody to the ideal Jerusalem, the heavenly city of purity. Such symbolic and psychological contrasts of place might remind the modern reader of Italo Calvino's *Invisible Cities* (1974, first published in Italian in 1972), a series of brief characterisations of cities, modelled on the perhaps equally imaginary *Travels of Marco Polo*.

We have considered the 'Who?', 'Where?' and 'When?' of the story; other questions one might ask, such as 'What?' and 'Why?', concern the *plot* of the narrative. What happens in the story? Why do such things happen in this way? Much of the narrative in a Gospel such as Mark's operates by conflicts between characters, and by religious controversies, which culminate in the passion narrative, describing the supposed trials of Jesus, his condemnation and death. But the sequence of events may be far from a straightforward historical sequence. As Elizabeth Struthers Malbon explains:

> Events are not always plotted in the narrative in the order in which they would occur in the narrative world. The changes from *narrative* world to the plotted time of the narrative are part of the implied author's discourse with the implied reader. Gerard Genette, a literary theorist, has worked out an intricate system for discussing the order, duration and frequency of events in the plotted narrative. An event may be narrated *after* its logical order in the narrative world (analepsis)[or flashback]. An event may be narrated *before* its logical order in the narrative world (prolepsis)[or anticipation]. And, of course, events may occur in the same order in both. An event may be narrated with a longer, shorter, or equal duration in comparison with its duration in the narrative world. An event that occurs once in the narrative world may be narrated once or more than once. Changes in order, duration, and frequency are ways the implied author has of leading the implied reader through the story-as-discoursed to an interpretation.
>
> (1992, pp. 32–3)

In Mark's story an obvious example of prolepsis is the threefold prediction of the passion, made by Jesus to his disciples within the story at Mark 8.31; 9.31; and 10.33. The writer of the Apocalypse seems to take much greater liberties with the temporal sequence of the narrative. The consequence of deforming the temporal order is sometimes known as the 'primacy/recency' effect. John alters the story by providing the outcome of the event *before* the event actually happens. The terrifying events are inevitable ('recency effect') but the writer has softened the impact by encouraging the readers to persevere and allowing them to glimpse a hopeful outcome beforehand ('primacy effect'). So Revelation 10 and 11 give assurance that God's people will be protected *before* the seventh trumpet is blown (11.15). The timing of events in the Book of Revelation has always been controversial. In the past this has often been a question of interpreting the sequence of happenings, and applying these to current events, so as to predict the end of the world. But it is also controversial from a literary perspective, in determining whether the events of the book fall on a straightforward time-line, or are part of a cyclic pattern with flashbacks and recapitulation. These matters are discussed in detail in the reading of Revelation by Alan Garrow in this Routledge series.

If we return to chapter 4 of Mark's Gospel, and read beyond the parable of the sower, we find in 4.26–29 a short parable about agricultural growth, which Mark obviously read as a kind of commentary on the original story of the sower. It is relevant to us at this point, because it makes its desired effect by means of a natural sequence of events in their logical order; if this happens 'of itself' (automatically), and we expect this to be so, then we should equally trust the dynamic of God's kingdom. The protagonists are the same as in the parable of the sower, but, whereas in that story we were told only that the farmer sowed his seed, here we are told that he scattered, slept, rose night and day, and finally put in the sickle. He was certainly not entirely inactive, but compared with the seed he was dilatory enough, for the seed sprouted and grew and produced automatically blade and ear and full grain in the ear. The point is not that we should imitate the farmer's lackadaisical approach to his future, but that we should discern the nature of the action which God's kingdom demands. That action is lit by the word *automate* ('of itself') and the guarantee that God is trustworthy.

Within the discourse about stories such as this, we are reminded of the importance in story-telling of the author's point of view. This is by no means to deny the value in creative possibilities of reader response to the story. But, as we have suggested, the interaction of readers and author, actual and implied, is part of the continuum of discourse that is the process of interpreting the story. Point of view certainly does not need to be a simple, single-minded attitude; it can be multi-dimensional and polyvalent, if not actually pluralist!

James L. Resseguie's study of the Apocalypse of John makes use of the four planes of point of view proposed by Boris Uspensky. These are the spatial and temporal, the phraseological, the psychological, and the ideological.

The Seer of Revelation distinguishes, on the *spatial* plane, between the perspectives of 'above' and 'below'; events that are seen to take place in heaven are used to interpret events on earth, or sometimes the other way round. On the *phraseological* plane John alternates between what is *heard* and what is *seen*. This enables him to indicate that the appearance of an event (what he sees) has another, deeper level of meaning (what he hears), or that what is heard (traditional expectations) is to be reinterpreted by what is seen (a new reality). The *psychological* plane employs contrasting images and symbols to transform the reader's understanding of events. We have already noticed the juxtaposition of the lion (traditional Messianic image) and the slain lamb (creative use of sacrificial image) to characterise the action of Christ in Revelation 5. In Revelation 12.7 the traditional imagery suggests that the archangel Michael wages war on Satan; but it is then revealed to the reader that the real power behind the victory is that of Christ ('they have conquered him by the blood of the lamb' – 12.11). In general terms, then, it can be seen that John's *ideological* point of view is essentially subversive; the implied reader's attention is focused not on the surface of the narrative, but beneath the surface, in order to be able to understand these events.

For the fullest understanding of a story one cannot overstate the importance of context, that is the immediate surroundings in which the author seems to have placed it, and the wider context of literary genre, both of which will in turn influence the reader. To illustrate the point, I cannot do better than echo the example which is quoted from G. Brown and G. Yule *Discourse Analysis* (1981) in Alan Garrow's study (1997) of Revelation in this Routledge series:

(1) A prisoner plans his escape
Rocky slowly got up from the mat, planning his escape. He hesitated a moment and thought. Things were not going well. What bothered him most was being held, especially since the charge against him had been weak. He considered his present situation. The lock that held him was strong, but he thought he could break it.

(2) A wrestler in a tight corner
Rocky slowly got up from the mat, planning his escape. He hesitated a moment and thought. Things were not going well. What bothered him most was being held, especially since the charge against him had been weak. He considered his present situation. The lock that held him was strong, but he thought he could break it.

(1981, pp. 139–40)

This same paragraph can be read in two different ways to communicate two distinct meanings. It strongly suggests that the context of meaning, established by the associated heading, influences and indeed determines the way the paragraph will be interpreted.

In conclusion, it is clear that we must gather all the information available from the context, and indeed ask about the original form of a story, before we set about analysing its structures and characteristics from the perspectives of new generation literary criticism. Historical and literary questions are far from mutually exclusive. With the fullest range of equipment, we are best prepared for the array of tasks that meets us, as we are caught up in the ongoing process that is the discourse about story.

Chapter 4

Intertextuality

This chapter will use a particular example to illustrate the different relationships which can be said to exist between one group of texts and two generations of readers. What these texts have in common is the theme of Anointing. While every reader may have a different response to texts, what distinguishes these two generations especially are the views they take on the legitimacy of holding a group of texts together in the mind. One generation may deny the very possibility, the other welcomes it as the only really creative response.

Our example concerns the Gospel stories of the anointing of Jesus; these are the texts: Mark 14.3–9; Matthew 26.6–13; Luke 7.36–50; and John 12.1–8. Other texts that could be considered in connection with these are Luke 10.38–42 (a meal with Martha and Mary at Bethany) and John 13.1–20 (Jesus washes the feet of his disciples).

1. ON HOLDING THE TEXTS APART

The question of the relationship between John's Gospel and the so-called synoptic Gospels (Matthew, Mark and Luke) has been debated endlessly by scholars. There tend to be changes of fashion, between the positive view of a limited and critical use by John of the others' written texts, the negative view which asserts John's effective independence, and what might be called the compromise position where John was a participant in a common tradition but had no literary relationship with the others. Fortunately this is not a problem that we need to solve before going further! But we should be aware of a prevailing view that minimises the historic links between the texts of the fourth Gospel and the other three.

This was not always the prevailing attitude. B.H. Streeter in his classic work *The Four Gospels* (1924) concluded: 'Clearly the facts so far stated amount to little short of a demonstration that John knew the Gospel of Mark and knew it well.' John has his own special Jerusalem traditions, and prejudices against Apocalyptic and Judaism. But 'the Gospels of Mark, Luke and John form . . . a series – Luke being dependent on Mark, and John on both the others' (pp. 400, 424f). Streeter's conclusions were widely accepted. But they were fiercely attacked in a revolutionary little book by P. Gardner-Smith *St John and the Synoptic Gospels* (1938). He argued that biblical critics had been preoccupied with a modest number of resemblances, and had ignored a range of significant differences. He asked whether 'it is easier to account for the similarities between St John and the Synoptists without a theory of literary dependence, or to explain the discrepancies if such a theory has been accepted' (1938, p. x). Gardner-Smith's work had enormous and persistent influence in favour of the independence of John, denying that John knew any of the synoptic Gospels as written works.

This is Gardner-Smith's discussion of the anointing story. He first lists nine points of similarity, in which John 12.1–8 might be thought to depend on the synoptic accounts:

1 The meal happens at Bethany (Mark 14.3).
2 John says that Martha served (Luke 10.38ff).
3 A woman anoints Jesus.
4 John uses Mark's phrase 'perfume made of pure nard' (cf.14.3).
5 John's word for 'very costly' is similar (the first half of Mark's word combined with the second half of Matthew's synonym).
6 A protest is made, and a price named of 'three hundred denarii' (cf. Mark 14.5).
7 John gives Jesus' reply as 'Leave her alone' using the singular verb where Mark uses the plural form.
8 There is a reference to 'burial'.
9 John 12.8 almost exactly agrees with Mark 14.7: 'You always have the poor with you, but you do not always have me.'

Secondly, Gardner-Smith provides a list of the differences:

1 John does not refer to Simon the leper (Mark 14.3); the natural inference is that it was Martha's house.
2 There are no grounds for the medieval identification of Lazarus with Simon, or the conclusion that Lazarus was a leper, in John 12.

3 According to John it was Mary, Martha's sister, who anointed Jesus. The synoptics do not say this, even in Luke 10.
4 John speaks of a very large amount of ointment ('a pound'). In pre-feminist days, Gardner-Smith concluded – perhaps correctly – that no woman could crush in her hand an 'alabaster jar' large enough to contain so much.
5 John says that Mary anointed the feet of Jesus, and wiped them with her hair; Mark that the woman poured the ointment on his head (but see Luke 7.38).
6 According to John, it is Judas who protests, not 'some' as in Mark or 'the disciples' in Matthew.
7 In John, Jesus' reply is different. The woman, it is suggested, bought the ointment to 'keep it for the day of my burial'. The woman is Mary, Martha's sister, but she is also thereby associated with Mary Magdalene.

(1938, pp. 45–7)

What is the best way of explaining this catalogue of similarities and differences between the 'anointing' stories in John and the synoptic Gospels? The only three precise correspondences in wording (listed as 4, 6 and 9 in the catalogue of similarities) could well be explained as stereotyped phrases within an oral tradition.

So Gardner-Smith concluded that the best solution was on the basis of a shared oral tradition and not as a literary relationship.

> John has taken the general account of the meal from the story of Simon the Leper, but he has introduced elements which belong to the picture of Martha and Mary and to the account of the meal in the house of Simon the Pharisee. Further, he has identified four different women with one another, the nameless woman of Mark, the sinful woman in Galilee, Mary the sister of Martha, and Mary of Magdala. . . . the improbability of his having done this if the Gospels of Mark and Luke were familiar to him can hardly be exaggerated. On the other hand, it is just the kind of thing likely to occur in a community still dependent on oral tradition.
>
> (1938, p. 48)

In the story of biblical scholarship this kind of detailed source criticism was swallowed up in the 1950s into a programme of 'redaction criticism'. This technique concentrated on the evangelists as individual writers, using their own selections of material (oral and written traditions) in order to express their own distinctive theologies, to preach the Gospel in their way, to reflect the religious needs of their own local communities. The author of the fourth Gospel had long been regarded as a personality in this way, largely because the theological difference of the Johannine tradition had been recognised widely, just as John's Gospel was known already in the late second century CE as the spiritual one.

Effectively, redaction criticism applied the same analysis of theological distinctiveness to Luke, Matthew and Mark in turn. They became theological teachers, not copy-editors, and their individual selection and arrangement of material was subjected to close and imaginative scrutiny. To illustrate the critical process, consider these words of John Fenton (from the 7th Eric Symes Abbott Memorial Lecture in 1992):

> Suppose someone comes along and says to you: I think I get the point of Matthew; it's all about impossible commands that are made possible because Christ is present with his disciples till the end of the world. I think I get the point of Luke; it's all about Christ the friend of sinners, and his offer of repentance and forgiveness; the parables are the main thing in Luke. I think I get the point of the Fourth Gospel; it's all about eternal life, and how you can have it now; this life is in God's Son; if you have the Son,

you have life. But, try as I may, I cannot see what the point of Mark is. I know he has more miracles per page than any of the other three; I know he hates the disciples; I know there is a problem about the end of the Gospel. In Mark, Jesus is remote; people are afraid of him and daren't ask him questions, and are always wrong whatever they say or do; and his own exit-line is My God, my God, why have you abandoned me? We never see him again after that. Tell me what to do, so that I can make some sort of sense of The Gospel according to Mark, because it does not seem to me much of a Gospel, a book of good news, at all.

As a result of redaction criticism such stories, with variations, as those of the anointing of Jesus became much less interesting collectively. The main focus was on the way Mark, for example, told the story, how it was distinctive, and how this story related to the overall structure and thematic purpose of his Gospel. The end result is four different stories of anointing, each with its own reasoning, with only occasional features that happen to overlap. To synthesise the four into one single harmonised account, in such a critical context, would appear improper and perverse.

With a range of examples to study, such as four anointing stories, one should try to elucidate the different emphases and meanings. If they are seen as different, but somehow historically related, which of them would be the original story from which the others are separate developments? One might take Luke first, as formative, arguing from the simplicity of the woman's gesture, seen as an act of homage to Jesus. There are a number of such instances where Luke's Gospel may preserve the original form of an individual story, even though the majority of scholars still believe that Mark's Gospel as a whole was the first to be written down.

In Mark's version there are further significant stages in the story. The woman's action is the only anointing which Jesus receives; it is regarded explicitly as anticipating the proper duty of preparing a corpse for burial. After Jesus' death, the women who come to perform this duty are forestalled by the fact of Jesus' resurrection. Without this woman's action, Jesus would have suffered the disgrace in Jewish eyes of burial without the last rites. The other development in Mark's story is the fact that the anointing is of Jesus' head, not his feet. There is at least the hint here of the act of anointing authorising the anointed one (the Messiah). Mark's picture of the Messiah is of one who fulfils the office by dying. So

Messiahship and death are linked together in this single highly symbolic action. In John's account it could be said that yet a further stage is added: uniquely here the woman is identified as Mary of Bethany, the sister of Lazarus, and the context of the anointing is as a sequel to the resurrection of Lazarus, the miraculous act by Jesus which anticipates Jesus' own resurrection.

2. ON READING THE TEXTS TOGETHER

A new generation of readers employs a wide range of techniques derived from secular literary criticism. The focus is probably on the reader and the responses which the reader made, or makes, in the process of reading. In the words of Robert M. Fowler:

> No longer can meaning be understood to be a stable, determinate content that lies buried within the text, awaiting excavation. Rather, meaning becomes a dynamic event in which we ourselves participate.
>
> (1991, p. 3)

It is not that the newly liberated reader sets out to flout past critical conventions by deliberately harmonising the texts of the four Gospels. Much more, the reader is concerned to identify and associate ideas within a creative response to the texts.

This association of ideas can be called 'intertextuality', in the sense of a relationship between written texts that is activated by the process of reading. Perhaps this should be seen in the context of chapter 2 on narrative theology, as a kind of sub-species of narrative criticism. These relationships between texts might be recognised for the first time by the modern reader as a wholly original response to the text. But they could have been recognised and documented by earlier generations of readers. The association of ideas could have been apparent to an early reader of the texts. The clues, to suggest the link, might have been planted by the original author of the work, or reteller of the story, so as to be identified by an implied reader (who is assumed by the author of the text). It is obvious that intertextuality can itself cover a range of meanings, from the premeditated purpose of the author to the spontaneous response of the reader. In the following illustration, we will concentrate mostly on the processes of reader response.

Before we see some of the advantages of this kind of intertextuality, it is important to look at the working assumptions of such a method. Often such an exercise proceeds hypothetically, by nominating a suitable 'first reader' of the text being examined, who will respond to the text in a predicted way. There are historical and social aspects of such reconstruction, making best use of available information; but it is also inevitable that, for example, a feminist theologian who selects a woman 'first reader' will characterise the response in accord with feminist perceptions.

The stories being considered in our illustration are stories where a woman plays a principal part (by anointing Jesus). It is certainly reasonable to propose, as 'first reader', a female member of the Johannine community, responding to the account of Mary of Bethany in John 12.1–8. Male and female readers may respond differently in a reading process that is both emotional and intellectual. A female reader, in such circumstances early in the life of the Johannine community, might well identify with a principal female character or adopt certain aspects as a role model.

To talk of 'first reader' means literally that she is reading the text for the first time and only knows what she has been told so far in the narrative. A second reading would have to take account of at least partial recollection. It is also usual in such an exercise to assume that the reader is informed, not naive, and has knowledge gained from other texts, as well as from membership of a Christian Church. An attractive idea, when thinking of such a reader in the Johannine community, is to propose that the reader picks up the clues placed by the author and uses the narrative of John's Gospel to define afresh those characters encountered earlier in the synoptic Gospels. Of course this is to assume that the author of the fourth Gospel was aware of such traditions in the other three Gospels. As we saw earlier, by no means can this be taken for granted.

In parallel to such a characterisation of the first reader and her reactions, such studies of reader response frequently consider a much later process of critical rereading. As we have seen, any reading after the first is inevitably different, as it reflects on the text with hindsight. One knows how the story ends, and experientially associates one story with a range of others. According to Wolfgang Iser,

> when we have finished the text, and read it again, clearly our extra knowledge will result in a different time sequence; we shall tend to establish connections by referring to our awareness of what is to come, and so certain aspects of the text will assume

significance we did not attach to them on a first reading, while others will recede into the background. . . . The time sequence that [the reader] realized on first reading cannot possibly be repeated on a second reading, and this unrepeatability is bound to result in modification of reading experience. This is not to say that the second reading is 'truer' than the first – they are, quite simply, different: the reader establishes the virtual dimension of the text by realizing a new time sequence. Thus even on repeated viewings a text allows and, indeed, induces innovative reading.

(1980, p. 56)

With the lapse of time, new readers bring to bear upon the text their own different experiences, and these begin to have a cumulative effect. A modern feminist theologian, for example, will read the biblical text against a background of a patriarchal society and with a sense of being a person oppressed by a male-dominated Church. To quote from Ingrid Rosa Kitzberger (whose work is used extensively in this illustration):

When I approach biblical texts I do so with a text already *written on my soul*, i.e., with my life-experience and my own story. Key is my socialization and history, as well as everyday experience, as a woman in a patriarchal and sexist society and Church.

(1994, p. 192)

What features of interpretation emerge from this method of associative reading? Here are some examples – neither a comprehensive list, nor a set of mutually exclusive options:

A. Reading John's Gospel for the first time, one first encounters Mary of Bethany at 11.2 ('Mary was the one who anointed the Lord with perfume and wiped his feet with her hair'). Someone rereading will know that the story is told in 12.1–8, but the first reader might be expected to recollect other traditions from the synoptic Gospels and associate these with Mary. The particular reference to wiping the feet might make a connection to Luke 7.38, since the stories in Mark and Matthew are both concerned with the head, not the feet.

B. At this stage no explanation is given for Mary's action. The suggestion is that such gaps in information to the reader are intended to trigger the process of intertextuality. John 12.7 will explain that the real purpose of buying the perfume was to keep it for the day of Jesus' burial. But, for the moment, the association with other synoptic traditions might indicate that the anointing anticipates the act of preparing Jesus' body for burial (see Matthew 26.12 and Mark 14.8; in Mark it *is* that act of preparation, and what is attempted in Mark 16 is faithless, in view of the resurrection prophecy – see 'just as he told you' in 16.7. Notice that in Matthew 28 there is no plan to anoint the body). It could even be said that Jesus is thereby the 'anointed one', and so the 'woman of Bethany' effectively acknowledges Jesus as the Messiah ('anointed'; cf. Martha in John 11.27). It is true that John uses a different word for 'anoint' in 11.2 and 12 from that Greek word preserved in the name 'Christ'; but given John's technique of working with balanced synonyms this will not prevent the association of ideas. In Luke 7 the motivation for the action is described differently ('she has shown great love' 7.47). But this idea too could carry over into the fourth Gospel's teaching on love. The cumulative result is that Mary of Bethany foresees Jesus' death, acknowledges him as Messiah, and loves him greatly.

C. The first reader of John's narrative, introduced to Mary of Bethany in 11.2, learns in the same chapter about her brother Lazarus's death and resurrection. Because of Jesus' involvement in such miracles, the Jewish council decides to put him to death (11.53). Now the reader clearly associates the deaths of Lazarus and Jesus. The actual narrative of John 12 begins with Jesus very much at risk of arrest, even in the house of his friends.

D. The association of John 12.2–3 with the story of Martha and Mary in Luke 10.38–42 reveals a different characterisation of the two sisters. John's story has a balanced equality between Martha and Mary, both sharing the initiative.

E. Another association with Luke 7.36–50 goes further than already indicated in B above. Mary's action, in anointing Jesus' feet with costly perfume, then wiping them with her hair, does not make best sense. Why wipe away the costly perfume? But seen in the context of Luke 7, the action makes more sense. There the woman is a sinner who wets Jesus' feet with her tears, and needs to dry them before applying the ointment (7.38). It could be intentional that John 12 is read in the light of Luke 7: Mary is seen as sharing the other woman's great love of Jesus, but (unlike her) she is *not* a sinner. The similarity and contrast together are signalled by the puzzle confronting the reader in the Johannine narrative.

F. In John 12 a contrast is established for the reader between Mary's dedicated action and Judas's complaint. The narrator prepares the reader (who remembers that Jesus is at risk) for Judas's future act of betrayal and also gives the reader an insight into Judas's corrupt character (12.4, 6). Judas is ostensibly worried about costly waste. By the time that Nicodemus and Joseph of Arimathea have spent an exceptional amount on spices for the burial of Jesus (John 19.39), Judas has done his worst (John 13.27ff; 18.2ff).

G. When Mary Magdalene goes to Jesus' tomb (John 20), there are aspects of her action which may well relate to Mary of Bethany and to the other women who attempted to anoint Jesus. The reader, remembering the story of Lazarus, might suppose that Mary Magdalene has gone to weep at the tomb, just as Mary of Bethany was expected to do at 11.31. While Mary of Magdala is weeping (20.11f), she looks into the tomb and sees two angels sitting where Jesus' body had rested, one at the head, the other at the foot. There is a real possibility of deliberate echoes here of those episodes when a woman anointed Jesus' head (Matthew and Mark) or his feet (Luke).

H. Far from being only 'minor characters' within the fourth Gospel, the women have a structural importance in the narratives. The reader who compares the roles of the female characters can reflect upon a development of theological ideas and of practical response to Jesus. A suggested pairing is between the Samaritan woman (John 4) and Martha (compare 4.29 with 11.27), and between Mary of Bethany and Mary of Magdala, who both find Jesus in the experience of death. The women are presented as positive models of response, those who seek to believe and understand.

I. Mary and Martha of Bethany offer examples of service, when they invite Jesus to a meal (John 12.2f). They, like the woman of Luke 7, are potentially – and probably intended to be actual – disciples of Jesus. The reader may recall the summary in Mark 15.40–1 about the women who 'used to follow him and provided for him'. Jesus' own programme and example to others is 'not to be served but to serve, and to give his life a ransom for many' (Mark 10.45). 'For who is greater, the one who is at the table or the one who serves? Is it not the one at the table? But I am among you as one who serves' (Luke 22.27).

J. Another story in John's Gospel exemplifies Jesus as one who serves at a mealtime: the footwashing in John 13.1–20. Jesus' action in washing the feet of his disciples is undertaken in full awareness of how near his death is. It is a symbolic act founded on proper hospitality and menial service. Mary of Bethany, when she anointed Jesus, performed an act of hospitality which Jesus interpreted in relation to his death and burial. The woman in Luke 7 washes Jesus' feet with her tears and then anoints them. Her action is seen as a substitute for the proper act of hospitality which should have been carried out by Simon the Pharisee (Luke 7.44–6). This woman, like Mary of Bethany, behaves like a truly hospitable host, in full accord with the example to be set by Jesus himself at the supper and on the cross.

K. During the footwashing, Simon Peter expostulates and rejects Jesus' action (John 13.6–8). This recalls the way that Judas complained about Mary's wasteful action in anointing Jesus (John 12.4ff; see F above). It also recalls Peter's confession of Jesus as Messiah (Mark 8.27–30), to be followed immediately by Peter's rejection of the very idea of the death which Jesus prophesies (Mark 8.31–3). This could be contrasted with the manner of Martha's confession that Jesus is Messiah (John 11.27).

L. Peter's expostulation is not the only negative reaction to the example Jesus sets. Many readers, if they are honest, might well feel acutely embarrassed at the role reversal (Jesus the master become slave) and the accompanying body language. It is important in rereading to reactivate the harsh paradox that an earlier audience or reader would have seen. An intertextual reading with Luke 7.36–50 is of assistance here. The woman in Luke 7 is a sinner; she enters the house of this Pharisee who strives to fulfil the Law and be sinless, in order that the Messiah may come. The woman touches Jesus in the most embarrassing way. The natural reaction is the Pharisee's: 'If this man were a prophet, he would have known who and what kind of woman this is who is touching him' (Luke 7.39). The Pharisee had hoped Jesus was a prophet; clearly he isn't, so Simon is acutely disappointed. In John 13 Peter resists the footwashing because he thinks he knows who Jesus is. 'Simon Peter thus reacts to Jesus' action just the way Jesus should have reacted to the woman's action, according to the Pharisee Simon. But here the "correct" reaction is just the opposite: non-resistance to and acceptance of this symbolic act' (Kitzberger 1994, p. 204).

3. INTERTEXTUALITY BETWEEN OLD AND NEW TESTAMENTS

It is well known or easily observed how often the New Testament writers quote from the Old Testament. This can be in the form of 'proof-texts', that is the authoritative statements with scriptural warrant from the Hebrew Bible, which are used to clinch an argument or establish a principle. But there are also many other, more allusive, ways in which Old Testament ideas and symbols are related to the Christian message. The situation affords great flexibility: there may be a choice between Hebrew and Greek versions of a text; the more appropriate or favourable reading is used, or the text may be adapted, or applied in a way which we would say was 'quoting out of context'. The driving force among these Christian writers was an overwhelming sense that earlier prophecies or religious prototypes had been fulfilled in the events of the life, death and resurrection of Jesus of Nazareth.

What Christians call 'the Old Testament', more strictly the Hebrew Bible or 'Tanak', was regarded as Scripture by Jesus and his contemporaries. In the first stages Christian writers did not think consciously of themselves as 'writing Scripture'. But they certainly saw themselves as interpreting Scripture, using methods that were comparable (but not necessarily identical) with those of the Pharisees or the writers of the Dead Sea Scrolls. They were practising consciously a kind of intertextuality by weaving such scriptural ideas into their own writings. In due time, perhaps in the next few generations of Christians, early readers of the New Testament writings would become aware of such intertextuality within the biblical 'canon', an interaction in progress between the two parts (Old and New Testaments) of a collection they regarded as equally Scripture.

It has sometimes been a subject for speculation among scholars as to how aware early Christian readers would be of the structural arrangement of the Hebrew Bible. The 'Tanak' (TNK) is so called because the initial letters sum up the contents of the three sections – Law ('T' for Torah); Prophecies ('N' for Nebhiim); and Writings ('K' for Kethubhim) – comprising the final collection. Did it matter from which of the three sections a Christian writer had drawn his 'proof-text'? A Jewish writer might regard the Law as most authoritative; some commentators assume that for a Christian the place of Law is overtaken by Prophecy. But there is some evidence that at least one early Christian writer – Paul – was concerned to give canonical support, balanced from all three sections, in his presentation of the Gospel of Christ.

This consciously tripartite Intertextuality in Paul can be illustrated at several points in his letter to the Romans. In Romans 15.4–13 (a passage appointed in the Book of Common Prayer of the Church of England to be read on 'Bible Sunday') Paul wrote:

> For whatever was written in former days was written for our instruction, so that by steadfastness and by the encouragement of the Scriptures we might have hope.
>
> (15.4)

> For I tell you that Christ has become a servant of the circumcised on behalf of the truth of God in order that he might confirm the promises given to the patriarchs, and in order that the Gentiles might glorify God for his mercy.
>
> (15.8–9)

This double statement of the fulfilment of the Old Testament in the Gospel of Christ is immediately supported by a chain (a catena) of proof-texts, drawn from

Psalm 18.49	Writings
Deuteronomy 32.43	Law
Psalm 117.1	Writings
Isaiah 11.10	Prophecies

Paul's arguments throughout Romans are strongly braced, by both authoritative quotations from the Law, and also prophetic texts drawn particularly from Isaiah. This is especially the case where Paul agonises over the relationship between Israel and the Christian Church, in Romans 9–11. In these chapters there are two instances of a structured arrangement of proof-texts from the Law, the Prophecies and the Writings. These occur at Romans 10.18–20 and again at 11.8–10. Paul would appear to be concerned to stress the interactive complementarity of his quotations. His argument seems to derive reinforcement from just this balance of authority within the canon of Scripture.

NOTE

The quotations at 10.18–20 are:

Psalm 18.5	Writings
Deuteronomy 32.21	Law
Isaiah 65.1, 2	Prophecies

and at 11.8–10 from:

Deuteronomy 29.3	Law
Isaiah 29.10	Prophecies
Psalm 68.23f	Writings

Here in strictest canonical order.

Chapter 5

Rhetoric

It's only performance art, you know, Rhetoric. They used to
teach it in ancient times, like PT. It's not about being right, they
had philosophy for that. Rhetoric was their chat show.

Tom Stoppard, *Arcadia*

It might seem that the area known as 'rhetoric' offers a level
playing-field on which those with historical interests in the New
Testament and those occupied with literary concerns in these texts
might engage each other on equal terms. For 'rhetoric' is an
essential category in modern literary criticism, which helps to
explain how any communication can succeed or fail; and 'rhetoric'
was an essential constituent of classical education in Greece or
Rome, a basic training in the skills of public speaking, applied to
careers in law and politics. But it soon becomes obvious that
historians and literary critics are not playing the same game with
rhetoric; they mean different things, and they play by different
rules, so the result of their encounter is confusion not clarity.

P.H. Kern, in a recent study of the scholarship on rhetoric, seeks
to clarify the situation by distinguishing four levels of talk about
rhetoric. The broadest level applies universally to any kind of
communication, so long as it can be said to be organised by
principles of strategy. In other words, the person who communicates desires to achieve a certain kind of result from the
communication; or, if it was not that deliberate, at least one could
observe with hindsight that putting matters that way was likely to
produce such an outcome. A second level of rhetoric applies
specifically to oratory, any kind of persuasive discourse, or the skill
to manipulate an audience. Here the principles used are not
necessarily rational; extremes of emotional manipulation or means

of bribery have been employed by demagogues throughout history. It should be noted that words are only one category of the material used in this kind of rhetoric.

When we come to the third and fourth levels of rhetoric, there the definitions apply to a geographically and historically restricted area – the world of Greece and Rome. The third level is defined in what is still a relatively general way, but it does apply particularly to the Graeco-Roman cultural milieu, that is the classical world of thought and its theoretical presuppositions and practical means of self-expression. The fourth level is the narrowest of all: namely, applying to the actual styles of discourse in Graeco-Roman society. This particularly refers to the handbooks for legal and political education which are our historical sources of information. They demonstrate the stereotyped forms that were taught as appropriate for set purposes. It is important to notice that such forms are not for all uses and all seasons; the contexts of use in law and politics are quite restricted; there are distinct styles, such as the judicial (for the law court), the deliberative (for the assembly or forum), and the epideictic (for ceremonial occasions such as funerals, games or festivals). Even Aristotle's work on rhetoric, often quoted in a general way, has in mind a particular application to politics.

In Kern's presentation we see how vital it is to distinguish the levels of talk about rhetoric. To confuse the levels, or slide between them, is to risk interpreting a particular game by a different set of rules. It may well be that the broadest level of meaning of rhetoric is originally derived from the narrowest level of the politics and law of Greece and Rome. But for purposes of meaning the new context is at least as important as, and probably much more significant than, any original root. The technicalities and particular rules of ancient practice are most unlikely to be carried over into the broader modern horizons of communication theory. Even less plausible is the idea that ancient rhetoric was controlled by theories of communication developed in the modern world.

CLASSICAL RHETORIC

Without blinding the modern reader with technicalities, it is desirable to give some impression of the nature of structural patterns and strategies employed in the public speaking of the classical period. The technical terms used for the arrangement (*taxis* or *dispositio*) of the elements within a speech are found in both Greek and Latin; in what follows only Latin terms will be mentioned.

A speech in the context of a court of law would usually have five main sections:

1 *exordium* or *prooemium* is introductory and ingratiatory;
2 *narratio* is the statement of the 'facts of the case' on trial;
3 *propositio* is a statement of the points that will be argued (if they are numbered points, it is known as *enumeratio*);
4 *probatio* is the actual attempt to prove the point/s;
5 *peroratio* is the summing up of the argument, accompanied by what is likely to be an emotional appeal to the judge.

An important aspect of a speech is the kind of strategy employed to strengthen the argument and to derive from it the maximum persuasive power. A common strategy was the use of 'common-places' (*topoi*), i.e. standardised features, in support of a case. These could include reference to parts of existing legislation (the quoting of case law); the development of an argument on the basis of the root meanings or etymologies of a key word; the use of a moral argument about the inherent value of something; or the citing of the letter of the law or its original intention. The aim is to move (in the course of the argument) from an opinion that is commonly shared, to establish the equal importance of a further opinion, or at least to persuade the hearers that it could be valid.

The classical handbooks were essentially guides to oratory, especially for the law court or the forum/assembly. They were concerned with fundamentally *oral* purposes. The celebrated Greek orator Demosthenes in the fourth century BCE wrote his speeches, both forensic and political, for public delivery. Cicero the equally renowned Roman orator, in the closing years of the Roman Republic, writing about the skills of oratory, says that Demosthenes had declared 'delivery' to be the most important, and perhaps 'the only virtue of oratory'. In such circumstances, the only real connection between ancient rhetoric and modern biblical study might be in the stress on the oral nature of the original communication which lies behind the biblical text. What really distinguishes ancient rhetoric from modern rhetoric is that the ancient techniques and usages were specifically designed for oral communication, while modern rhetorical analysis is applied essentially to the literary styles and structures of a document.

Seneca declared that oratory, as a formal and public skill, is to be distinguished from conversation:

> I prefer that my letters should be just what my conversation would be if you and I were sitting in one another's company or taking walks together – spontaneous and easy. . . . Even if I were arguing a point, I should not stamp my foot, or toss my arms about, or raise my voice; but I should leave that sort of thing to the orator.
>
> (*Epistulae Morales* 75)

It is equally obvious that rhetoric, as oratory, would exclude second-order disciplines such as philosophy and epistemology, and the tools and methods of analysing a text. But it is true that there were other ancient types of rhetoric, not those of the training handbooks, which could be used by those who were not orators by profession. For example philosophers, including sophists, would make use of certain techniques in discourse, to be more effective in winning adherents.

Jan Lambrecht writes about rhetorical criticism and the New Testament:

> Rhetoric is the art of persuasive speaking. Since all biblical texts are to some degree persuasive texts, a knowledge of rhetoric is part of the equipment of the exegete. Rhetorical analysis, then, constitutes one of the exegetical tools.
>
> (1989, p. 239)

This seems like an uncontroversial introduction to a study in which Lambrecht has made valuable contributions, full of insight, to biblical exegesis. But it should be observed that he makes a shift from a general point, at the second level of defining rhetoric, to a justification for employing the tools of the fourth and narrowest level of understanding. At the level of the classical handbooks, rhetoric is about construction, not analysis, and concerned with speeches, not texts. Modern critics need active vigilance to guard against reading back what are presuppositions of their critical processes into the criticism of the ancient world.

To quote from Edward P.J. Corbett's textbook *Classical Rhetoric for the Modern Student*:

> From its origin in Fifth Century Greece, through its flourishing period in Rome and its reign in the medieval *trivium* ['a place where three ways meet' in the liberal arts of grammar, rhetoric

and logic], rhetoric was associated primarily with the art of oratory. During the Middle Ages, the precepts of classical rhetoric began to be applied to letter-writing, but it was not until the Renaissance, after the invention of printing in the Fifteenth Century, that the precepts governing the spoken art began to be applied, on any large scale, to written discourse.

(1990, p. 20)

Again we are reminded of the dangers inherent in a casual crossing of the boundaries of understanding; we mistake the rules of the game we are playing and may mislead others thereby.

Much of the consideration of classical rhetoric in relation to the New Testament has been focused on the letters of Paul, particularly Galatians, parts of the Corinthian correspondence, 2 Thessalonians and Philippians, as well as Romans. A recent study of Romans by J. Moores has examined what are known as 'enthumemes' in the letter. These rhetorical motifs also fascinated Archbishop Lanfranc in the eleventh century CE. But this does not mean that scholars are universally agreed on their identifications of particular types of rhetoric in each of these letters. Even among those who have concentrated on the types of classical rhetoric from the handbooks, Galatians is labelled as judicial rhetoric by Hans Dieter Betz, but as deliberative rhetoric (from the political assembly) by George A. Kennedy.

Since Galatians exists for us in the literary form of an epistle/letter sent by Paul, it is at least questionable whether it should be regarded primarily as a classical oration. Even if in the past a letter was designed to be read aloud, and clearly represented in writing something of what one would have expressed orally if one had been present, or again if it was thought appropriate to preserve a celebrated speech in a literary form for posterity, already the simple fact of the literary form has created some distance from the concept of a public oration. The processes of editing into a text, and of subsequent revisions to what was said, inevitably make a difference. It is fundamental, however, to a case such as that of H.D. Betz that Galatians is not just an epistle which can be analysed with the assistance of rhetoric, but it is an actual oration. It conforms to the conventions of a speech, according to Graeco-Roman rhetorical principles.

It was mentioned earlier that other types of rhetoric, not those specified in the handbooks for legal and political training, were used in philosophical argument by such as the sophists. David Aune uses this kind of model in his interpretation of Paul's letter to the Romans. He discusses the rhetorical form of *logos protreptikos* and declares that 'Romans is a speech of exhortation in written form' (1991, p. 91).

Stanley K. Stowers (1994) employs a similar model in his *A Rereading of Romans: Justice, Jews and Gentiles*. Paul uses the 'protreptic' form in which to introduce himself to a new audience and – because he is serious and not just polite – to build in a warning to his readers against their prevalent vice. In their concern for moral self-mastery, Paul's Gentile readers believe that they have found a successful aim through Jewish teaching in the Law. Instead Paul seeks to persuade them that it is God's action in the person of Christ which meets their real need. When Paul presents his own Jewish identity (as in Romans 9), it is to show how God has actually stalled Israel's restoration in order to make room for Gentiles. Paul's favoured concept of 'weakness as strength' is culturally at home in this Graeco-Roman discourse on the theme of self-mastery.

Stowers seeks to recover the original nature of the text of Romans from centuries of Church use as a general letter and as a normative theological treatise about Christianity (neither Jewish nor pagan but a 'third race'). His chosen way to recover the original is by applying literary and rhetorical patterns from the period of writing. The reader needs sensitivity to rhetorical conventions such as 'speech in character' (a device to dramatise the cut and thrust of an argument in dialogue).

In the same way the reader is made aware of coded references to cultural ideas, prevalent at the time. While Paul obviously quotes frequently from the Old Testament, he can also refer to a theme from Greek tragedy (e.g. Euripedes' *Medea* at Romans 7.15, 19). Greek prowess in athletics was one of Paul's favourite images for use in metaphor. Stowers also suggests that in Paul's day the polarisation of Jew and Gentile functioned in a similar way to the classic contrast between Greeks and barbarians.

Such cases for the identification of Paul's methods of argument in the patterns of classical rhetoric are strongly argued and often illuminating. But we are a long way from scholarly consensus. For every identification in the realm of rhetoric, there are at least an equal number of attempts to relate Paul's argument to the techniques of Jewish exegesis of Scripture, in the Diaspora or at Qumran. Theories about ancient rhetoric are often blended with ideas from modern literary theory. Such crossing of the boundaries (so well defined by P.H. Kern), and the positing of eternal truths in an area so open to changing fashion as the literary world, leaves plenty of room for doubt.

RHETORIC AS NEW LITERARY CRITICISM

Within the realm of literary criticism as applied to biblical texts, the scholar widely acknowledged as the pioneer of rhetorical criticism was James Muilenburg. He introduced his ideas in an article entitled 'Form Criticism and Beyond' (1969). This shows how the techniques emerged as a reaction against some aspects of form criticism, rejecting its tendency to ignore the actual content of a text because of preoccupations with standard forms and structure. Instead Muilenburg advocated that special attention be paid to the distinctive and unique features within any formulation. Then the critic has an internal involvement with the text, rather than generalising about it from an external perspective.

Muilenburg's technique was termed rhetorical criticism, although it has been suggested it would be better to call it 'stylistics', to avoid the confusion with classical rhetoric. The method is to concentrate on the effect upon the reader of the rhetorical devices and structural patterns within the text. This is to understand 'rhetoric' at the second level of Kern's classification – that is, the manipulative means employed in a persuasive discourse. It does not depend upon the identification or resurrection of classical patterns. But it is a strictly literary discipline ('new literary criticism') which brackets out all historical considerations. In the words of Adele Berlin: 'if we know *how* texts mean, we are in a better position to discover *what* a particular text means' (1983, p. 17).

A good example of the method at work is in Joanna Dewey's studies of the Gospel of Mark. She analyses in detail selected portions of the Gospel to demonstrate how the surface patterns and literary structures of the text convey both the themes and the plotting of the argument. 'It is the task of the rhetorical critic to educate and sensitize the reader/hearer to the experience of reading – or listening to – the text of the Gospel of Mark.' The first reading is a linear presentation of the individual units of Gospel material. The second reading is a representation of the rhythm of a section of the text, taken as a whole. Dewey describes a concentric structure within the Galilean controversy section (Mark 2.1–3.6), linking themes of sin, fasting and sabbath observance, and developing an association of ideas between eating and discipleship. The individual units of the text, identified by form critics of the previous generation as surviving fragments of oral preaching, are now shown to be interrelated, by compositional characteristics, as part of a literary pattern.

Rhetorical criticism of this kind goes further than redaction criticism (with its emphasis on the Gospel writers as compilers and theologians); by analysing the process of construction and composition it shows how the force of the argument is achieved. This represents a revolution in literary attitudes, particularly as far as Mark's Gospel is concerned. A reader who begins from a position of some scepticism about the literary character of Mark, or about the literary sensitivities of the evangelist's first audiences, would be amazed at the transformation.

Leslie Houlden expressed this well:

> Scarcely used in the Churches until only the other day, Mark's revival is owed to critical scholarship. A hundred years ago, it seemed that, if [Mark came] first, it must be more reliable, giving us something like a simple life of Jesus. No great shakes as either theology or literature, its value lay in its proximity to roots. So what a revolution have we now seen. In the past thirty years, one heap of books opens up Mark's theological profundity, another explores its extraordinary literary qualities. Whoever thought there was such depth, such refinement here?
>
> (*Times Literary Supplement*, 15 January 1993)

Further evidence of changing perspectives is supplied in the recent work of Elizabeth Struthers Malbon. In 1938 R.H. Lightfoot's *Locality and Doctrine in the Gospels* was published. This was a radical work in its day, an historical study of Gospel composition, using the insights of form criticism. Lightfoot argued that Mark's Gospel represented Galilee as the sphere of divine redemption, contrasted with Judaea as the world of antagonism and disaster. Nearly fifty years later, Elizabeth Struthers Malbon carries forward many older insights, including Lightfoot's, in *Narrative Space and Mythic Meaning in Mark*. But her interest in the composition of Mark is literary rather than historical. She studies the interrelationships of no fewer than 288 spatial references in the Gospel, adapting for the purpose the structuralist methods which Lévi-Strauss used to analyse myths.

Malbon incorporates much else besides references to place, and rightly so, for spatial organisation is only one aspect of Mark. She discusses three broad categories of references: geopolitical (e.g. Nazareth in Galilee – 1.9); topographical (e.g. the other side of the sea in 5.21); and architectural (e.g. the Capernaum synagogue – 1.21). She begins by setting out the detailed facts, then traces the narrative sequence, and finally analyses the structural scheme.

Malbon seeks to demonstrate how the underlying oppositions (which are identified according to the structuralist principles) – familiar/strange; promise/threat; profane/sacred – are mediated or broken down. Ultimately the three pairs of categories are reintegrated within the overall opposition (order/chaos). For this the key principle of mediation is discovered in the prophecy at 16.7 that Jesus 'is going ahead'; he is already 'on the way', where 'way' (Greek *hodos*) is 'more an action than a place'. In Malbon's expression, 'a way between places, a dynamic process of movement' does indeed sum up the storyline of Mark's Gospel; at the same time it is the way that Mark's community, receiving the communication in their particular situation, seek to resolve their own experience of conflict.

These kinds of 'new literary criticism' often refer to the literary design of the examined text as its 'rhetorical structure'. This embraces a range of matters, such as overall plot, author's point of view, the ways characters are portrayed, the uses of symbolism and numerical arrangements, and staged conflicts and polarisations within the text, often employing irony and the device of misunderstanding.

One of the most stimulating guides to these matters is the American scholar Stephen D. Moore. In his *Literary Criticism and the Gospels: The Theoretical Challenge* (1989) he observes, 'Today, it is not our biblical texts that need demythologizing so much as our ways of reading them' (p. 66). Moore offers a map of the landscape of criticism and a guide to the ways of reading, describing the developments in literary theory since the days of structuralism. The two sections of the book concentrate respectively on plot (the structural composition of a narrative), and the role of the reader. Stephen Moore's own recommendation is for a strategy in reading to combine toughened versions of narrative criticism and of reader-response criticism. But his book is not presented as a straightforward introduction for beginners in modern literary criticism; it resembles an interlocked series of critical book reviews, as the author sets up a sequence of debates conducted between pairs of attitudes which he analyses and polarises for us. Thus the argument is structured to proceed by binary oppositions, until the end.

Not for the first time one notices that the theories employed by a writer in modern composition are the same theories that are applied to ancient texts. Listen to Bas Van Iersel, in his unpublished narrative commentary on Mark, commenting on the issue of Jewish food laws, with reference to Mark 7.14–23:

> Perhaps most important of all, the author of Mark presents this and other issues in the form of opposites, using contrast and emphasis to dramatize the difference between the favored and the rejected position. The same applies to the way he portrays his characters. A case in point is the contrast between Jesus and the disciples, which has become apparent before and is also present in this episode, namely when Jesus in verse 18 rebukes them in terms reminiscent of 6.52 for their opacity. . . . Before long the contrast between Jesus and the disciples will find expression in a criticism more severe than anything directed against any opponent (8.33).

It is immediately apparent what a different view is being maintained of the essentially literary construction of Mark's narrative, compared with the fragmented impression of the text in the older commentaries (such as Vincent Taylor in 1952) based on the principles of historical criticism and form criticism. But there is also a distinction to be recognised between two varieties of the modern (and holistic) view of the evangelist's narrative.

Firstly, composition or redaction criticism focuses on the content of the narrative, and the theological reasons for the evangelist's selection and combination of the material. This is a development from the inherent tendencies of earlier biblical study, to use the text as a *window*. Through this window the historical situation of the evangelist and his community may be glimpsed; or by this means an historical message may be appreciated for itself and then transferred to the modern world, where it is applied (essentially as allegory) to a new and different situation. For a discussion of the social relativity of a particular text see chapter 6, and for an examination of allegory see chapter 8.

Secondly, narrative or new literary criticism focuses on the form and plot of the narrative, the rhetoric and literary devices of the text. This approach is based on techniques borrowed from (secular) literary studies: the readers are urged to read Mark's Gospel just as they would any other story, attending to the internal world of the story and the interplay of its characters. The text is thereby used as a *mirror*, in which the concerns of the reader, ancient or modern, are equally reflected. These readers see their own immediate situation represented directly in the argument of the text. So they can learn the message of the text for their own time.

In the most comprehensive kind of biblical interpretation, a dichotomy between the use of a text as a window or as a mirror may sound arbitrary and false. An interpreter may be equally interested in how a text was and how it is; the historical and literary approaches may not be mutually exclusive options. But the distinction still has a useful function, in clarifying some essential presuppositions, and indicating practical differences of priority in working methods.

Composition criticism and narrative criticism both share an holistic preoccupation with the idea of an overarching purpose, the concept of an author in control of the text. The difference between the critical methods is that in composition criticism the idea of the author is authentic, while in narrative criticism this is called the 'intentional fallacy' – the notion that the meaning of a literary work is identical with its author's intention. It is questioned how much an author could control the text and the ways in which it is read, for the author's own time, let alone in the future. If, from the interpreter's vantage point, the simple realism of an author in control of the text is exposed as naive, then the literary process of composition needs to be analysed in a much more sophisticated manner.

The most influential treatment of this problem is Seymour Chatman's model of narrative communication, set out in his *Story and Discourse* (1978), and extensively applied to biblical texts (e.g. to John by R. Alan Culpepper in *Anatomy of the Fourth Gospel*, 1983, and to Matthew by Jack Dean Kingsbury in *Matthew as Story*, 1986). The basis in literary criticism is a theory of narrative rhetoric: everything in the narrative discourse is selection, framing, arranging, filtering, slanting, that is, essentially a matter of rhetorical skills. Culpepper describes his application of the theory:

Our aim is to contribute to the understanding of the Gospel as a narrative text, what it is, and how it works. . . . By 'how it works' I intend questions regarding how the narrative components of the Gospel interact with each other and involve and affect the reader.

(1983, pp. 5–6)

Chatman (1978, p. 151) represents the model of narrative communication diagrammatically (see Figure 5.1). Communication from the real (historical) author to the real (actual) reader proceeds, according to this theory, by means of the rhetorical chain of persons included within the box labelled 'Narrative text'. Stephen Moore explains the diagram as follows:

> Distinguished from the flesh-and-blood author is the *implied author*. This term denotes the complex image of the real author that the reader infers as s/he reads – a selecting, structuring, and presiding intelligence, discerned indirectly in the text, like God in his/her creation. The author's generation of this textual second self is a profoundly rhetorical act (e.g. Luke 1.1–4). The *narrator* is also said to be immanent in the text as the voice that tells the story, a voice which may or may not be that of one of the characters. The principal New Testament examples of narrators who do participate in the story as characters are John of Revelation, and the 'we'-narrator of Luke–Acts (see Acts 16.11ff). The narrative voice is the instrument by means of which the story-world, and the image of its author–creator, is transmitted (a bearer of divine messages, if you will). The *narratee* is defined as the narrator's immediate addressee (e.g. Theophilus in Luke–Acts), and the *implied reader* as the (generally more oblique) image of 'the reader in the text': the reader presupposed or produced by the text as (in some theories) its ideal interpreter.
>
> (1989, p. 46)

With renewed emphasis on reader response (that is on the reader affecting the text directly by the process of reading, rather than simply being told by the authorial voice what to think) Chatman's

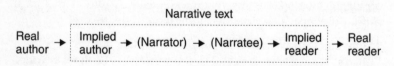

Narrative text

Real author → Implied author → (Narrator) → (Narratee) → Implied reader → Real reader

Figure 5.1

diagram may require some modification. The place for reader participation needs to be more explicitly indicated, perhaps by some two-directional arrows.

An interesting example of this direction of discussion is provided by Bas Van Iersel, in a Dutch article the title of which translates as 'His Master's Voice: The Implicit Narrator in Mark, the Voice and the Figure':

> The question raised by the closing verses of the Gospel of Mark . . . is whether the implied author/narrator of Mark's Gospel, that has been passed down to us anonymously, and that has no narrator telling Jesus' life story, can be given not only a voice, but also a shape.
>
> Do the young man near the grave (16.5–6) and, retrospectively, the young man in Gethsemane (14.51–2) and the possessed of Gerasa (5.18–20) stimulate the reader to form an image of the narrator? . . . Because these characters, just as the narrator, function as a messenger, the reader can recognize characteristics that he may apply to the narrator.
>
> Through these narrative figures, the reader sees in the narrator a second-generation Christian (14.51–2) who takes his mission from Jesus (5.18–20) whose message he repeats (16.5–8), and therefore, who can be called 'his master's voice'. He is also someone who has failed, who has run away (14.52) in the moment of trial. If the book is written for Christians in Rome who have failed during Nero's persecutions, then this is another reason to listen to this voice.
>
> (p. 127)

SOCIO-RHETORICAL CRITICISM

One of the most free-ranging of New Testament investigations to speak in terms of rhetoric is the work by Vernon K. Robbins entitled *Jesus the Teacher: A Socio-Rhetorical Interpretation of Mark* (1992). As the title suggests, this work builds a bridge between rhetoric and sociological studies. Robbins is concerned that justice is done to the cultural influences of Greece and Rome upon the New Testament documents, balancing these with the root ideas from the Old Testament and Judaism. He uses the term 'socio-rhetorical' to indicate how 'a well-known social environment in the culture could play a key role in the rhetoric of a literary narrative'. He studies the social environment of the relationship of teacher and disciple. Mark's Gospel is regarded as tracing the 'socio-biological life-cycle' from the beginning to the end of Jesus' direct relationship as teacher with his disciples.

The primary influences on Robbins seem to be the methods of role theory and social anthropology. The rhetorical considerations, by comparison, are rather general and volatile. But they have their impact in the literary shape of the Gospel and its parallels. Both Xenophon and Mark portray the teacher (Socrates and Jesus respectively) as accepting the sentence of death which the deity requires; the legal process involves the local courts, but the injustice of the death is what is most remembered. Robbins concludes:

> The rhetorical form of Mark's Gospel reflects a time when both Judaism and Christianity were adapting to a new cultural milieu that was emerging in the Mediterranean world. The Gospel of Mark represents a group of early Christians who were taking Jewish ideals away from established Jewish tradition and participating in the well-established cultural streams of tradition in eastern Mediterranean culture. . . . The members of this group did not have prestigious social status in major urban centers. Rather, they performed a respected role among people throughout towns and villages in eastern Asia Minor, Syria and Palestine. In the role of the itinerant teacher–healer, they had a ready-made avenue into the village-town culture. . . . They understood themselves to be followers of an itinerant teacher who gathered disciple-companions and refused to violate the system of thought and action when he was rejected and killed. . . . They found an integrated life as they focused their identity and energy in mission by means of a particular selection of values and patterns of action from both Greco-Roman and Jewish society and culture.
>
> (1992, pp. 212–13)

This description leads us neatly into our next area of study, a chapter concerned with the text in a social context.

Chapter 6

The text in a social context

The letters of Paul are real letters, written to particular Churches, at a particular time, to meet a particular situation, by a particular man who believed in particular things passionately. The letters are first and foremost 'occasional documents' in the sense of timely writings, called up out of Paul's interest and concern for the Churches in his care, many of which he had founded.

To understand the letters properly we always have to get to know something about the writer, about the people to whom he is writing, and especially about the social background to the local problems and concerns with which he is dealing. Otherwise it resembles overhearing or listening to only one side of a telephone conversation. We hear but we do not understand, unless we are already party to the issues discussed. This would be true of all ancient and modern writings of this kind, and it is specially true of Paul's letters. This is *our problem* with the letters of Paul; we need to know the issues in the local situation and we often have to reconstruct the other side of the conversation from what we hear Paul saying. For the letters of Paul must never be approached in a vacuum, but always as living writings addressed to living situations. Only then, perhaps, can one go on to appreciate them as letters that have become part of the New Testament.

To illustrate this I shall concentrate on Paul's first letter to the Corinthians, because it is so typical of Paul's 'problem-centred' approach. Paul appears to write his letter in response to a long list of questions and difficulties which have emerged in this Church. The issues have been raised; Paul feels compelled to respond; and he teaches the Church about matters of faith and practice – effectively he does his theology – by the way he responds.

But in order to take an overview of these problems in the Pauline

Churches, some of the main problems have been arranged under four headings, which can give a sense of life in the Christian community from first to last. The headings are: joining the Church; living together; growth; death and resurrection.

1. JOINING THE CHURCH

The act of joining the Church, then in Corinth as often nowadays, is symbolised by a ceremony of initiation, the event of Christian baptism. The scene can be set in first-century Corinth, making use of a vivid and well-researched reconstruction in Walter J. Hollenweger's *Conflict in Corinth* (1982):

> On the following Sunday morning Tertius awakened me at three o'clock in the morning. A full hour's walk lay ahead of us. We set off. As it was still dark we took oil lamps with us. We left the city and walked up through an olive grove. When we arrived at the top of the hill we were able to blow out our lamps as the stars had begun to fade. Between the leaves of the olive trees one could visualize the sea rather than see it.
>
> We walked on, left the path and descended into a gorge. We could hear the river roaring, and soon we came upon a basin which the river had carved out in the rock over the centuries. It seemed as if the water turned around in a circle, partly flowing underneath the rock. About thirty to forty Christians stood at the water's edge facing the rock. Tertius and I remained at a respectful distance because he was not sure whether or not the Christians, and in particular the baptismal candidates, would be embarrassed by the presence of an outsider. As the service took place in the open air, they could not altogether avoid being seen by passers-by. However, as Tertius explained, there was nothing secret about baptism.
>
> I saw that Red Chloe was there with some slaves and foreign workers. I also noticed Crispus, the former chairman of the synagogue. Chloe's people sang a beautiful morning hymn:
>
>> Awake, sleeper,
>> Rise from the dead,
>> And Christ will shine upon you.
>
> They sang it several times, and with each stanza they added new harmonies. Then one of the slaves – Fortunatus – walked into

the water. Suddenly there was a total silence. When the first rays
of the sun slanted down into the basin, all the Christians sang
'Halleluja, Jesus is Lord.' Then the baptismal candidates were led
to Fortunatus. He cried aloud, 'Jason, I baptize you in the name
of Jesus. Amen.' He immersed him in the river and the Christians
shouted, 'Amen!'

The candidates were wrapped in white gowns and rubbed
dry. Fortunatus said to them, 'Baptized into union with him, you
have all put on Christ as a gown.' The Christians left singing.

(1982, pp. 15–18)

Such would have been the rite of baptism in the early years of the
Corinthian Church. Remember that there were no purpose-built
Churches. Baptism would have taken place in the open air, at a
riverside. And each individual Christian congregation would have
numbered about thirty or forty – no more than fifty because of a
very practical reason. If they met indoors they would have to meet
in somebody's house, probably the house belonging to a wealthy
member of the congregation who functioned as a patron of the
group.

But baptism was the cause of problems in Corinth, as can be
seen by contrasting 1 Corinthians 1.11–15 with 1 Corinthians 6.11:

For it has been reported to me by Chloe's people that there are
quarrels among you, my brothers and sisters. What I mean is that
each of you says, 'I belong to Paul,' or 'I belong to Apollos,' or 'I
belong to Cephas,' or 'I belong to Christ.' Has Christ been
divided? Was Paul crucified for you? Or were you baptized in the
name of Paul? I thank God that I baptized none of you except
Crispus and Gaius, so that no one can say that you were baptized
in my name.

(1.11–15)

Some of you used to be [wrongdoers of all kinds]. But you were
washed, you were sanctified, you were justified in the name of
the Lord Jesus Christ and in the Spirit of our God.

(6.11)

Paul makes the point that there is only one undivided Christ. If you
are baptised in the name of Christ (as would have been the regular
practice at this time), if you have him and belong to him, then it is
trivial whether you attach yourself to Paul, Apollos or Cephas.

Conversely, no devotion to one of these human teachers can make up for not having Christ. The problem was that, in the ancient world, if you joined a secret society or a mystery religion, you would owe a special debt to the teacher who initiated you, and hold to a special relationship with him. It is like a modern cult, where there can be passionate devotion to one's teacher or guru. This seems to have been the problem in Corinth; at least some of them thought that Christianity was this kind of secret cult.

Paul stresses that the Corinthian Christians belong to Christ. Paul's primary task is not to baptise but to preach the Gospel:

> For Christ did not send me to baptize but to proclaim the Gospel, and not with eloquent wisdom, so that the cross of Christ might not be emptied of its power.
>
> (1.17)

But it is possible that there was another problem with baptism, for the Corinthians and for other Christians, in the way that Paul talked about the theology of baptism in relation to the death of Christ. The famous text is Romans 6. 3–5:

> Do you not know that all of us who have been baptized into Christ Jesus were baptized into his death? Therefore we have been buried with him by baptism into death, so that, just as Christ was raised from the dead by the glory of the Father, so we too might walk in newness of life. For if we have been united with him in a death like his, we will certainly be united with him in a resurrection like his.

If we find this powerful and striking, but very difficult, theology – perhaps the Christian converts who listened to Paul felt the same. The metaphor relating baptism to dying, and particularly to the death of Christ, would have intensified the sense that Christianity was like one of the ancient mystery cults.

2. LIVING TOGETHER IN THE CHURCH

> Brothers and sisters, I appeal to all of you in the name of our Lord Jesus Christ to agree with one another in what you say, so there may be no divisions among you, and all of you may be united in a common mind and purpose.
>
> (1 Corinthians 1.10)

We have already seen potential causes of division within the Church at Corinth. There is the problem of achieving a real unity overall when Christians meet, for practical reasons, in small house-churches. There are difficulties when allegiance to a personal teacher, who perhaps baptised a whole congregation, might distract attention from Christ himself. And there are obvious social problems, when a small congregation contains some slaves and very poor people, as well as a wealthy householder, civil servants and state officials. Social divisions may be inevitable, even at a Church meeting for the Lord's supper, when some bring food and others rely on charity, and when the owner and his friends gather in the dining room, leaving the others outside in the hallway and courtyard. There may be reverberations also when an outspoken woman like Chloe is involved.

We should not exaggerate these social causes, but neither should we minimise their effects. Would a radical social mix fare any better today in our supposedly 'classless society'? It remains true that Paul's first words, after the opening formalities of this letter to the Corinthians, are concerned with a significant lack of agreement within the Church of Corinth. These words are in the emphatic position where we would naturally look for the theme of the letter. And it is this lack of agreement which Paul strives to remedy in the course of this letter.

Many of the issues discussed are matters of Christian practice and ethics, where differences clearly exist over the proper conduct, behaviour and customs for Christian believers. In short, how should they live together within the Church?

1 Is it proper for a Christian man to live with his father's wife? Should the community acquiesce in such behaviour? (1 Corinthians 5)
2 Is it proper for Christians to take legal actions against other members of the Church? What are the appropriate sexual ethics? Should a Christian make use of a prostitute? (1 Corinthians 6)
3 In view of the expectation of the world's end and the imminent return of the Lord, is there any future in the marriage relationship for Christians? How should husband and wife behave? (1 Corinthians 7)
4 Is it proper for an individual Christian to eat any meat or food that has been offered in the temple of a pagan god before it was put on sale in the market? Should the Christian eat a meal in a pagan home? Or be seen eating with unbelievers in a restaurant next to the temple precincts? (1 Corinthians 8–10)

5 Is it appropriate for women, who already lead worship in the house-churches of Corinth, to disregard the widely prevailing social norms concerning dress and public speaking? Should the wealthy members of these urban Christian communities insulate themselves from the poor when they come to celebrate the Lord's supper? Is it proper for an individual or a group, endowed with special gifts, so to monopolise the practice of Christian worship as to exclude others from taking part? (1 Corinthians 11–14)

These are some of the problems in Corinth which threatened harmonious relations. What is the relationship of the individual to the group? Is there need for the community as a whole to agree upon an ethical pattern of behaviour? In general we can conclude firstly that nobody worked harder for the unity of the Church than Paul did. There is no way that Christ can be divided. But secondly we conclude also that nobody endangered the unity of the Church as much as Paul did.

How might one make this second claim? The reason is that Paul may have endangered unity by preaching a Gospel of freedom. As Ernest Best writes:

> He was not primarily concerned to calm his converts down, when they were excited and distraught, but rather to speak the truth as he saw it, and encourage them to do God's will.
>
> (1988, p. 8)

3. GROWTH TOWARDS CHRISTIAN MATURITY

The problems in Corinth, and elsewhere, concerned issues of belief as much as matters of practice. See, for example, 1 Corinthians 3.1–2, where Paul says,

> I could not speak to you as spiritual people, but rather as people of the flesh, as infants in Christ. I fed you with milk, not solid food, for you were not ready for solid food. Even now you are still not ready.

After the topic of meat from pagan temples, you might think that 1 Corinthians is very largely concerned with food. Here in chapter 3 we have milk or meat. That immediately might suggest the Jewish kashruth, the dietary regulations and practices: not milk products and meat in the same meal. For Paul this is the source of the metaphor, but not the source of his meaning.

In modern terms, we might think of the prescribed diet (to help you to lose weight and be more healthy) on one side, and the fast food or the 'takeaway' on the other. The subject is two different kinds of eating. But the real contrast is between two different attitudes of mind about eating. Here it is the metaphor which changes, and with it the associated attitudes of mind which Paul says must be altered.

The Corinthians spurn Paul's Gospel. This milk of his is the equivalent of baby food; it seems an 'elementary' idea, because he concentrated simply on the death of Jesus on the cross. What the Corinthians want is real meat, something to get their teeth into. They have found this 'meat' for themselves, in advanced philosophical speculations and the esoteric kinds of wisdom.

Paul's point is that they are trying to be too clever, to run before they can walk. When they become mature adults, ready for proper food, then Paul can offer them true wisdom, what the world regards as the 'folly' of the Gospel. But when they are really mature Christians, the Corinthians will realise the full meaning of the Gospel of Christ. It will be seen as the same Gospel of Christ crucified which Paul preached. Then the Corinthians will realise that they do not need any other type of food. To quote from Morna Hooker, to whom this discussion has been indebted:

> In seeking the wrong kind of wisdom, the Corinthians have split the Church into cliques [sects] and turned their backs on the true wisdom, which is a total reliance upon God. They have shown that they are still babes, for they have not yet grasped the implications of the basic truth of the Gospel – 'Christ crucified'; until they realise that the scandal of the Cross has put an end to all human boasting, they will be unable to digest the diet which is offered to the mature.
>
> (1990, p. 105)

4. DEATH AND RESURRECTION

Early Christian belief about Christ centres on the cross and the resurrection. When Paul writes to the Corinthian Church about their particular problems in belief, especially with the doctrine of the resurrection, he begins with a kind of summary creed which the early Christians shared, a statement of the essentials of faith:

For I [Paul] handed on to you as of first importance what I in turn had received: that Christ died for our sins in accordance with the Scriptures, and that he was buried, and that he was raised on the third day in accordance with the Scriptures, and that he appeared . . .

(1 Corinthians 15.3–8)

By reading widely in his letters, we can appreciate how Paul understood these clauses of the creed. We can see how he places special emphasis on certain points, perhaps more than other Christians would have done in the early years. What we might find most difficult, however, is discovering how the Corinthians would understand the death and resurrection of Christ. This is *our problem*, which we may only be able to solve by reading between the lines of Paul's argument, and by reconstructing what it is that he is arguing against.

Belief in the resurrection of Christ has often posed problems. Was it a matter of finding the tomb empty, as the Gospels say? Or was it a series of visions, experiences of the risen Lord, as Paul seems to suggest here? But actually, if we read on to 1 Corinthians 15.12, we discover that the Corinthians' problem with the resurrection was not the same as our modern scepticism:

Now if Christ is proclaimed as raised from the dead, how can some of you say there is no resurrection of the dead?

We gain the impression that the Corinthian Christians wanted to understand Christ's resurrection differently. They agreed with Paul in affirming that Christ was raised from the dead. But they wanted to understand Christ's resurrection independently of any general doctrine about the future resurrection of all Christians, while seeing themselves as *already* effectively 'raised' because they are 'wise' and 'spiritual' people. Paul's response was to try to make them see how empty this renders the Christian faith.

If there is no such thing as a general resurrection of the dead, then Christ himself was not raised from the dead. You need to be able to see the Christian proclamation about Christ in the light of the much wider idea of the future raising of the dead at the last day. Paul stresses that these ideas stand or fall together, and he devotes 1 Corinthians 15.21–57 to a complex series of explanations. If there is no idea of resurrection, and therefore no proclamation of the resurrection of Christ, then Christian faith is empty because resurrection is an essential part of it.

But for Paul this emptiness of the Christian without the risen Christ is idle and rhetorical speculation. The affirmation of Christ's resurrection is central to the creed shared by early Christians. Christ's resurrection stands as a pledge. That is sacrificial language for the payment of a first instalment which guarantees the ultimate payment of the total. Because Christ is raised, the resurrection of the rest of humankind, or at least of those who are in Christ, is assured.

The resurrection of Christ is a particular example to demonstrate how the possibility of a general belief in resurrection may be justified. A difficulty here is that one cannot simply generalise on the basis of one particular instance. But Paul does not leave the resurrection as just a general possibility. He goes further by referring to his own theological understanding of the meaning of Christ's death and resurrection. The chapter is a collection of separate arguments from which Paul draws a triumphant conclusion. Christ's resurrection carries with it the application of its significance to each individual Christian in a whole range of ways. 'For as all die in Adam, so all will be made alive in Christ' (15.22).

Conclusions

This working example has involved looking at a range of problems in the Pauline Churches. In the space it is not possible to do more than try to offer a representative cross-section of the issues. We have concentrated on 1 Corinthians because it is such a striking example of the 'occasional' letters of Paul, written to deal with a whole set of local problems in a particular social context. But it would be equally possible to look at other letters in a comparable way.

The material was arranged in four sections, so as to group it for analysis. It covers the full length of the Christian life, from first involvement to future hope for the individual. And it is concerned with problems in Christian practice and behaviour, as much as with difficulties in belief and doctrine.

The fact that this treatment of Paul's letters is problem-centred must not lead us to conclude that Paul's Churches had nothing but problems. Perhaps we should end with a quotation from Philippians in order to redress the balance:

I thank my God every time I remember you, constantly praying with joy in every one of my prayers for all of you, because of your sharing in the Gospel from the first day until now. I am

confident of this, that the one who began a good work among
you will bring it to completion by the day of Jesus Christ.

(1.3–6)

* * *

In much the way that Walter Hollenweger did in *Conflict in
Corinth*, one should append some observations about the
substance and method of such a treatment of the text in a social
context. In these areas of studies in the social sciences it is all too
easy for the relevance of the method to be overwhelmed by
discouraging jargon. I hope my treatment in more general terms
will prove more helpful.

Corinth was the third city of ancient Greece, after Athens and
Sparta. Excavations on the site show a high level of civilisation from
the fourth century BCE. Like Athens, the site of the city is dominated
by an acropolis on which were temples, including a notorious one
to Aphrodite, goddess of love. The Romans razed the city to the
ground in 146 BCE, after a period of revolution; Corinth was rebuilt
by Julius Caesar one hundred years later. Under Augustus it became
the capital of the Roman proconsular province of Achaea.

The city's chief asset was its location on the western end of the
isthmus of Corinth. It was well placed to control trade, both north and
south (from central Greece to the Peloponnese), and east and west
(across the isthmus). Before the Corinthian canal was built (finished
in 1893!), the arrangements for portage from Lechaeum on the
Corinthian Gulf to Cenchreae on the Saronic Gulf spared shipping the
much longer and more dangerous voyage around the south of the
Peloponnese. So Corinth flourished as a centre of trade and industry.

A modern observer anticipates certain social consequences in
such a prosperous trading centre. Corinth was certainly cosmopolitan – which gave it appeal, presumably, to Paul as a centre of
mission – but its image as the 'sin capital' of the ancient world is
disputed. There is actually a Greek verb 'to live as in Corinth'
meaning 'to have a sexually liberated lifestyle', but this was a satire
of Aristophanes on the Greek city and does not inevitably apply to
the Roman colony. But there was a proverbial expression – 'not for
every man is the voyage to Corinth' – which must have given Paul
pause for thought.

It is reasonable to ask what the preaching of Christ's Gospel
would mean in a Hellenistic/cosmopolitan city like Corinth. If

possible, one should try to get into the skin of a person in the Corinthian marketplace, or tanner's workshop, who heard Paul speaking of a crucified Lord who was now alive and offered new life in a new fellowship with new hope. What would induce the Corinthian to abandon the Lord Sarapis, for example, in favour of the Lord Jesus? It is important to recognise that the discussion does not happen in exclusively theological terms, but has human and social aspects. All kinds of human thoughts and motives will have been involved.

Non-Christians writing in the ancient world about Christian groups tend to see the Churches as tiny, peculiar, anti-social, irreligious sects, drawing their adherents from the lower strata of society. Classical writers called Christianity a 'superstition'. Basically they meant it was foreign and strange, like the religion of the Celts or the Egyptians, at least when compared with the piety of traditional Roman observance to the gods of the state. It could be feared like a mystery cult of the most extreme kind (such as the Bacchics), or it could be suspected as being politically subversive like a secret society or a revolutionary political group.

It has often been assumed that Christianity has always been a movement of the lowest classes of society, just as when Jesus worked with fishermen and tax collectors. But the evidence, as presented for example by Wayne Meeks in *The First Urban Christians* (1983), shows that the situation was much more complex. It may well be true that a Christian Church was close to being a cross-section of society, even including some 'yuppies'. While the teaching of Jesus originated among the country people of Galilee, the world of Paul and his Churches is the world of the city. Studies of the situation in Corinth reveal leading figures in the Christian groups who belong to quite high social and economic levels. The conflicts in the congregation are largely conflicts between people of different social strata.

The Christian Church needed its wealthy patron. There were no special buildings in which the community or cell groups could gather. So they either met in the open air or went by invitation to a house that was sufficiently large, owned by a wealthier member of the community. It would be natural for the person who owned the meeting place to assume, or be accorded, a leadership role as the patron of the group. Clearly the use of a 'house-church' would place constraints on the number of people who could worship together. In a city like Corinth there were likely to be several house-churches, doubtless producing rivalries and cliques on occasion.

As an illustration, one of four houses of the Roman period discovered by archaeologists in Corinth is the villa at Anaploga (see Figure 6.1), the structure of which belongs to Paul's time. Unless a separate room was used as a chapel (as in the later villa at Lullingstone in Kent, or in the baptistery of the house-church at Dura Europos), the community would gather in the public rooms. At Anaploga this would mean the triclinium (dining room) which measures 7.5 × 5.5 metres – 41.25 square metres of floor – and the adjacent atrium (courtyard) measuring 6 × 5 metres – although here the effective floor area is less than 30 square metres because of the usual impluvium (pool) in the centre.

The nature of the religious competition in the world of Corinth can be suggested by a comparison with the temple of Asclepius, the god of healing, at Corinth (see Figure 6.2). The comparison can only be general because it is uncertain how much of the fourth-century BCE construction, apart from the temple proper, was rebuilt by the colonists in 44 BCE. Pausanias described the site as a place of refreshment in summer. The association of ideas about a religious location can be indicated by a quotation from Vitruvius's treatise *On Architecture* (1.2, 7) dealing with the criteria for temples of healing:

> For all temples there shall be chosen the most healthy sites with suitable springs in those places where shrines are to be set up, and especially for Asclepius and Salus, and generally for those gods by whose medical power sick persons are manifestly healed. For when sick persons are moved from a pestilent to a healthy place and the water supply is from wholesome fountains, they will more quickly recover. So will it happen that the divinity (from the nature of the site) will gain a greater and higher reputation and authority.

The principle still held good for the siting of Cistercian monasteries in the Middle Ages!

Developments of techniques and theories in social archaeology greatly assist in the interpretation of biblical sites, including the landmarks of biblical archaeology. The importance of the criteria governing the interpretation of material evidence, including inferences about social organisation, societal values and religion, cannot be overstated.

A good illustration – but a long way from Corinth – is the pool of

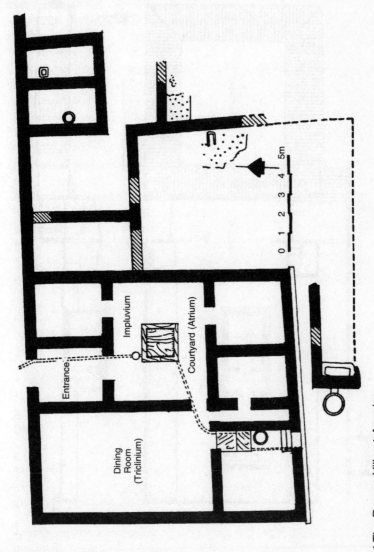

Figure 6.1 The Roman Villa at Anaploga

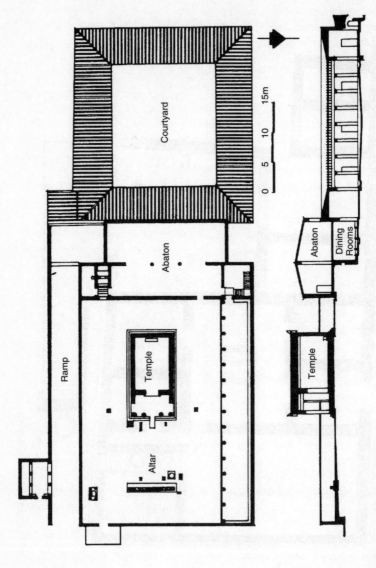

Figure 6.2 The Asclepion at Corinth

Bethsaida in Jerusalem, referred to as the setting for the healing in John 5. The traditional methods of biblical archaeology would use the facts from the partial excavation of the site to reconstruct the design of the pool and relate this to what John 5.2 describes as 'five porticoes'. Nowadays more penetrating questions can be asked. The archaeological evidence is that a pool on this site had a reputation for its healing properties right through into the second century CE in the rebuilt city of Aelia Capitolina. Over the years, before and after the New Testament period, there was such a significant commitment of building materials, land and planning to the pool of Bethsaida that it is possible to infer its importance in the value system of ancient Jerusalem. Bethsaida held a high, officially sanctioned position in this society's system of values.

Archaeological data are necessarily fragmentary and unsyste-matic, prior to interpretation. But houses and tombs reveal much about social roles and status. Building materials and the amount of space in a house indicate rank and prestige; the arrangement of a graveyard mirrors social arrangements just as positively as the employment of professional sculptors on a tomb shows high status. The nature of trade and information networks reveals as much as coinage does about a particular culture. The fact that Jesus is recorded in the Gospels as avoiding the regional hubs of trade networks, places such as Sepphoris, Tiberias and Caesarea, must have a positive significance.

We acquire information about different kinds of location in which New Testament events happen; this information from social archaeology must in turn colour our understanding of the events. Locations are personal or public or sacred; some locations are in between the public and the private, not completely in either category. This is sometimes called 'meso-space'. The best example of personal space is normally a private house. So in Mark 2.1, when Jesus is 'at home' in Capernaum, the crowds gather, but one would expect Jesus' own private space to be inviolate; when four men dig through the roof (2.4) on behalf of a paralysed man, this is a shocking intrusion into personal space.

Public space is a city marketplace or a village courtyard; anything that happens here is public knowledge and may acquire public notoriety. A good example of meso-space would be a synagogue. As far as we know, a synagogue was intended for the heads of households; so events that occur there are not quite public, but neither are they simply private. The events in a synagogue might be called elitist or even oligarchic. When Jesus exorcises a demon in the synagogue, at Mark 1.23ff, we must see this as a pivotal event which would affect village and probably also regional attitudes. The temple is obviously sacred space, and it must be significant that Jesus taught there (e.g. Mark 11.15ff; 12.41ff). On the one hand, the location in the existing sacred space of the society must seem to add gravity to the impact of Jesus' teaching and actions upon the audience. On the other hand, one could argue that the Gospels effectively redefine sacred space, from the existing priority of the temple and its hierarchy, to the local house-church and the personal space of the individual and the small group (modelled on the twelve disciples).

This chapter has examined 1 Corinthians as an exemplary text from which one can learn much about the social context to which it applies. We have also approached the social context from the historian's perspective, considering what we can know of an environment from historical records and from interpreting archaeological remains. To study the social context, using a range of methods, can yield the best of both worlds, historical and literary, for the reader's benefit.

In conclusion, it is helpful to reflect upon the functions of any text, such as the New Testament documents, from both its literary and its social aspects. Elizabeth A. Castelli expressed these ideas succinctly and well in her study *Imitating Paul: A Discourse of Power* (1991):

> Literary studies tend to focus on patterns of representation and various forms of audience analysis, trying to take into account how a text might be received and the variations among audiences. Sociological studies, on the other hand, tend to use the text for what it can reveal about the culture that produced it and tend not to read the texts as literary objects.
>
> (1991, p. 38)

She claims that it is possible and desirable to effect a combination (or one might say a compromise) between the literary and the sociological study. Her own work is 'positioned in the space between these two types of scholarly investigation' and 'acknowledges that *both* social forms *and* the discourses that construct and sustain them are central to the creation of new social meanings'. For this double consciousness one could compare a study such as

Burton L. Mack's of the Gospel of Mark, *A Myth of Innocence: Mark and Christian Origins* (1987). Castelli observes:

> When I read the New Testament, I see a complex struggle taking place over social forms and meanings. A new interpretation of power is being produced, located in a matrix of emerging social relations and articulated through self-referential claims to authority. [It is necessary to question] how early Christian language and social organization are tied to early Christian *ideas* about texts and social formations. In other words, how are modes of organizing social life bound up with the production of texts that explain them? Such an investigation requires a dual focus on what is said, and what is not said, about this relationship.
>
> (1991, p. 38)

Chapter 7

Psychological readings

Symbols are prisms through which people or peoples look – or
are taught to look – at reality.

Amos Elon, *Jerusalem*

There is a current and exceedingly stupid doctrine that symbol
evokes emotion and exact prose states reality. Nothing could be
further from the truth; exact prose abstracts from reality, symbol
presents it. And for that reason symbols have something of the
many-sidedness of wild nature.

Austin Farrer, *Rebirth of Images*

The method of psychological reading sits more comfortably
alongside the sweep of narrative criticism and theology than ever
it could have done with earlier methods of source analysis or the
most fragmenting deconstruction. Why should this be? Jonathan
Magonet expresses it well:

I remember a discussion with a Rabbinic colleague who was
reviewing a new book on the Bible. It was written from a
psychological perspective and he was most irritated with it.
'How can you psychoanalyse the figure of Abraham in the Bible
when the stories all come from different sources?'

I can understand his annoyance. Having committed himself to
source criticism it was difficult to have some newer critics
trampling all over the theory and reading the texts as a 'unity', let
alone unleashing psychology on them.

Yet, having been committed to a literary approach to the
Hebrew Bible for years I find myself particularly interested in
where the line can be drawn in such an exercise.

(1992, p. 11)

What is true of Judaism and the Hebrew Bible is equally true at least of traditional Christian scholarship of the New Testament.

A psychological reading will see the story in the text as a totality. It will be argued that the best way to understand a story of the New Testament (or the Old Testament) is to consider it as a human story with sophisticated narrative techniques at play. All characters in the story – including Jesus Christ and God himself – are equally open to the process of psychoanalysis. For some readers the act of considering God as a character may seem almost blasphemous. But this way of looking at the (human) interactions between the whole cast of characters in a story may prove to be especially fruitful. One is responding to the human voices within these stories, and thus also to the human voice of the narrator. We can hope to see what the narrator sees and also the reasons why.

A central concern of psychology is to reveal (and perhaps to explain) an individual consciousness. What is consciousness? What is the self? Daniel C. Dennett (1992) recently offered a rather unattractive description of it as 'spatio-temporally smeared all over the brain'. Is there a single subject of consciousness, or even a single stream of consciousness? Dennett argues instead for multiple channels, different parts of the brain, whose functions together make up what is called consciousness.

An interesting analogy that is suggested is that of the modern academic text. As a result of the various technological revolutions that are word-processing, desk-top publishing and electronic mail, it is quite possible for there to be multiple drafts of an academic article all in circulation simultaneously. Some may incorporate corrections and fresh additions; others may include responses to comments made on the first draft. It would be entirely arbitrary to seize on any one of these versions and pronounce it to be the canonical text. Similarly, to seize just one moment in the brain's processing and call it consciousness would be equally arbitrary. If this analogy can be sustained, we should also notice one incidental effect: it may make it more possible for psychology to cope with the multiple versions of a story from different sources.

One of the thought-experiments which Dennett uses to support his case is a party game called Psychoanalysis. One player goes out of the room, having been told that, while she is out, another player will relate a dream to the remaining guests. When the first player returns, she is told that she is only allowed to ask yes/no answers in order to discover the dream. Then she has to psychoanalyse it and identify the dreamer. But there is a hidden catch. The questioner does not know this, but the party guests must answer 'yes' if the last letter of the question is in the first half of the alphabet, and 'no' if it is in the second half. There is also a non-contradiction rule which overrides such answers as might conflict with earlier ones.

Here is a sample of how the game might proceed:

Q. Is the dream about father?
A. No.
Q. Is it about a telephone?
A. Yes.
Q. Is it about mother?
A. No.
Q. Is it about father, really?
A. No.
Q. Is it about father on the telephone?
A. Yes.
Q. I knew it was about father! Now, was he talking to me?
A. Yes.

There are two points about this game as an illustration: firstly we see how the questioner herself creates the story, and secondly consciousness in this way is not wholly driven by the data.

There are many major figures in the story of the rise of modern psychology, but the two giant influences in this field are Freud and Jung. This chapter will look at some possibilities of New Testament readings that are influenced by Freud and Jung respectively.

FREUD, THE PSALMS AND THE HYMNS OF THE BOOK OF REVELATION

It has long been recognised that Revelation, although it belongs to the literary genre of apocalyptic writing, includes within itself a wide variety of other literary forms. Among these are the liturgical hymns, many of which resemble the Old Testament Psalms in form, style and language (see 4.11; 5.9–14; 6.10; 7.10–12, 15–17; 11.15–18; 12.10–12; 15.3–4; 16.5–7; 18.10–19; 19.1–8). The deliberate nature of this relationship to the Old Testament is demonstrated especially in Revelation 15, where the song is ascribed both to Moses and to the Lamb (15.3). It is the song of Moses because much of the imagery recalls Israel's Exodus from Egypt (see Exodus 15); and it is the song of the Lamb (that is, Christ himself – see Revelation 5.6) because victory was achieved through Jesus' own sacrificial death on the cross.

The words of the song (15.3–4) are a skilful amalgam of Old Testament quotations. It sums up the Old Testament vision of God as the king to whom all nations come (Micah 4.1–3). This could be regarded by Israel in a rather nationalistic way (Isaiah 49.22–3; 60.10–16). But in Revelation the martyr-throng beside the sea of glass expresses a confidence in universal salvation, of which they are the 'first fruits'.

The hymns in Revelation are by no means all triumphant or triumphalist. There are indeed other hymns of praise to God (5.9–14; 19.1–8), and distinctive songs of thanksgiving (11.17–18). But there are also expressions of comfort in grief (7.15–17) and impassioned outpourings of lamentation (6.10; 18.10–19). These hymns cover the spectrum of human religious experience, just as the Old Testament Psalms do.

Ideas from Freudian psychotherapy can help us to understand the relationship of lamentation to the rest of religious experience: it can be seen positively as a vital stage in approaching God, rather than negatively as a bewailing of what one is lacking in religious experience. Walter Brueggemann in a study of the Psalms of Lament writes: 'Israel moves from an *articulation* of hurt and anger, to *submission* of them to God, and finally *relinquishment*'. These Psalms are making a statement in the context of prayer to God and petition.

According to the principles of Freudian talk-therapy, human beings do not move beyond the level of repressed memory unless they speak it aloud to someone with authority who hears. The idea of one-to-one therapy of this type can be extended to a collective practice in both social and liturgical contexts. Effectively a religious covenant with God (such as Israel's with Yahweh), without a proper place for lamentation and articulated memory, becomes nothing more than a practice of denial and pretence.

A further dimension of understanding is suggested by D.W. Winnicott, a neo-Freudian dynamic psychologist, in his study *The Maturational Processes and the Facilitating Environment* (1965). He claims that a child develops ego strength and object relationships by taking the initiative with its mother, and so experiencing a kind of omnipotence. For this to work, the child's own actions require a responsive disposition from the mother and not excessive initiative from her. In the same way the religious believer can be seen as taking the initiative in the practice of lamentation. It would suggest that the truest understanding of the human self also requires that discernment of God as one who is willing and prepared to be a respondent.

If we apply this directly to a reading of Revelation, the text to which it relates most immediately is 6.10. The souls beneath the altar do not merely engage in a protest movement. By their articulated cry they express not only a grievance but also a knowledge of God who can and will respond. Revelation 18.10–19 is the lament of those implicated in the evils of Babylon, as they observe God's judgement. In a traditional interpretation no more need be said than that the guilty losers receive their due deserts. But one of the worrying aspects for modern readers of Revelation is the lack of opportunity for repentance, or even due warning of ultimate judgement. Did they have a fair chance? With this more open reading, informed by psychological insights, one could see the act of lamentation as providing just that moment for approach to God and a positive divine response.

JUNG, JOB AND THE JOHANNINE SYMBOLS

Carl Jung (1875–1961), reacting against the faith (or blind obedience) of his father who was pastor of Basel Reformed Church, argued for the immediacy of religious experiences leading to knowledge. The Bible can easily become an obstruction, inhibiting critical thought. But the Bible is full of numinous images. The psychological forces of the unconscious ('archetypes') can be attracted into consciousness by biblical images, and thereby provide psychic healing and stability. In addition, for those psychologically well developed, the Bible can act as a mirror reflecting the forces of the unconscious, and this may lead to 'individuation' as the goal of psychic development.

It is clear that what is involved is a process of spiritual and psychological transformation. The Bible's function is then not primarily to provide information (e.g. on religious history); rather its importance lies in the text's deeper levels of meaning, where hidden messages can still be discovered. A non-believer may actually be in a better position than the believer to interpret these messages with profit. In such readings the process of 'active imagination' (dreaming with the eyes open) is stimulated to greater activity. This is a psychic process which must be kept distinct from the artistic ways in which it is often given expression.

Jung himself gave a good illustration of the process at work in an essay, written as late as 1952, entitled *Answer to Job*. He claimed to have discovered three important but hidden meanings of Scripture, through his encounter with the text of the Old Testament book of Job:

1 God is not only good, but also evil (darkness as well as light);
2 God, like man, seeks higher consciousness and individuation;
3 God is present in human beings, and to be discovered in their inner lives.

In effect the analytical psychologist is here 'putting God on the couch'. God becomes aware of his own shadow, his own dark side. The act of incarnation (God becoming man) is seen by Jung as a kind of compensation to man for the wrong done to Job. It also enabled God to catch up with man psychologically, and thus facilitate his own individuation process. But the Christ of the Gospels seems effectively to repress the divine shadow in his perfect goodness. To recognise the antagonism of opposites is a feature of consciousness; then the task is to integrate the opposites. At a lesser level, I wonder if Jung would have approved the intention in the 1996 performances of the mystery plays at York not only to cast God as a woman but also to have Satan played jointly by a man and a woman?

In the New Testament, the book of Revelation can be regarded as a theological attempt to integrate the opposites of good and evil. Here we see the wrathful side of God functioning alongside the God of love. Jung writes:

> The purpose of the apocalyptic visions is not to tell St. John, as an ordinary human being, how much shadow he hides beneath his human nature, but to open the seer's eyes to the immensity of God. . . . For this reason he felt his Gospel of love to be onesided, and he supplemented it with the Gospel of fear: God can be loved but must be feared.

But this integration is incomplete in Revelation. According to Jung, what is required is a continuation of Christ's incarnation, and this is to be found in the Holy Spirit, the Paraclete, as promised in John's Gospel (John 14.15). This is God in the unconscious of man. The process of redemption depends upon a divine-human collaboration, rather than the submission of humanity to the omnipotence of God.

Jung's own views are clearly influenced by his personal psychology (the influences both of his father and of Freud). His Christianity becomes a form of analytical psychology. But Jung's openness to the ideas of John's Gospel might encourage us to look a little further in this direction. One of the most fruitful aspects of psychological reading of texts is its sensitivity to symbols.

The modern world has become more critically aware of symbols and their potency, from the logos of business enterprise to the political value of images such as the demolition of the Berlin Wall or the Statue of Liberty replicated in China's Tiananmen Square. Such symbols may not always have the desired effect, or are open to different interpretation. The symbol's advantage, and its risk, is precisely its multiple associations. Consider, for example, a Church of England dictionary of theological concepts which have been translated into sign language for the deaf. 'Hosanna' becomes clenched fists whirled around the head; 'devil' is the index and little finger of the hand raised to represent horns; and 'Easter' is a crossing of the hands as in 'hot cross bun'.

The use of symbolism in John's Gospel is well known; Johannine themes, such as water, bread, light, shepherd and vine, have often been used as a pattern for Religious Education courses, not least because they are readily accessible at several levels of understanding. In studies of the fourth Gospel such symbolism has been variously defined: by its historical background in the life of Jesus or the Church; for its structural importance as giving literary shape to the whole; in its social function as identifying or unifying a group; or as offering an existential self-understanding of the Christian, possibly in contrast to a Jewish self-understanding.

These definitions of symbolism fall broadly into two categories: firstly, where the Gospel text functions as a window, so that the reader can look through and see John's Church as it was; and secondly, where the text is a mirror, to enable readers to see themselves. Beyond this, the value of a psychological reading of the symbolism of John's Gospel rests in the fact that psychology provides a link between the two functions of the text as window and mirror. If we ask what is the psychological function of the Johannine symbols, we are seeking to know how these symbols functioned for Christians in the first century, and at the same time how they function for us today. The psychological question effectively adds the unconscious to the conscious, producing and observing the interaction between them. In Gerd Theissen's words, psychological exegesis 'seeks to describe and explain human experience and behaviour' (1987, p. 1). Or, to quote Walter Wink: 'We have analyzed the text; now we may wish to find ways to let it analyze us' (1978, p. 141).

In the language of the fourth Gospel, the Johannine symbols bring together the world above and the world below. In Jungian terms, they relate the unconscious and the conscious. The traditional language of the other world, of height and transcendence, is associated with, and perhaps translated by, the interior language of psychology, of depth and immanence. This is to stretch further what John Painter wrote in terms of existentialism:

> The symbols, derived from the world of sense experience, are used to communicate that which transcends the world in order that the transcendent might be *experienced*.
>
> (1979, p. 35)

Michael Willett sums up the contribution of Jungian psychology in this way:

> A symbolic reading of the Fourth Gospel from the Jungian perspective, then, would see the Johannine symbols as symbols of transcendence, which reconcile unconscious and conscious, the world above and the world below. The Gospel's symbols, like dream symbols, are interpreted through amplification and association, that is through exploration of the symbol's significance in the contemporary literature and through consideration of the personal meanings the symbol has for the reader today. In the context of the Johannine community, these symbols functioned as compensation for the trauma of excommunication from the synagogue, so that the symbols of Judaism were reappropriated in terms of the new symbol of the Self, Jesus.
>
> (p. 13)

There are obvious dangers if a method of biblical interpretation becomes too closely attached to a passing fashion of study in another discipline. This risk may well be greatest in the field of psychology, given the fierce competition between methods and the rapid changes in theory, even in the present century. The case of C.H. Dodd and his interpretation of Paul's argument in the letter to the Romans chapter 7 can illustrate the problem. This chapter may be read at an intensely personal level, as if it were Paul's own confession. But if the letter to the Romans is regarded as more of a systematic theology, then Paul's statement resembles a theological statement developed on the basis of general principles about God and his human creation.

In the 1930s C.H. Dodd wrote two articles entitled 'The Mind of Paul' which offered a psychological interpretation of Romans 7.7ff. as Paul's vivid personal recollection. Paul had begun life in a secure position in the cosmopolitan society of his time. But the self-consciousness of the strict Jew was deeply engrained as a result of his upbringing. Such circumstances provided a battleground for acute internal conflict between the two faces of the same man, Saul the Jew and Paul the Roman. To the end of his life it must have remained a miracle that Jew and Gentile could ever meet on common ground.

According to Dodd's reading, Paul psychoanalyses himself as he recollects the stages of his life. As a little child his instincts were unrestrained. As the boy matured, his instincts began to be repressed with his consciousness of sin and commandments. This repression was accepted inwardly and became a basis for confidence, celebrating the Law as the glory of Israel. The personal factor of excellent achievement (see Galatians 1.14) was then added to the impersonal pride in the glory of Israel. The ideal was one of scrupulous perfection; thereby the larger concept of Law (Torah) was narrowed to concern for particular commandments. Here was vast scope for inner conflict, as natural passions were repressed by a fanatical ideal. As Galatians 1.14 and Philippians 3.4–6 also reveal, Saul engaged in a violent persecution of the Christian Church. Essentially it could be said that he was externalising his own inner conflict, by means of attacking the outsiders, those declared enemies of the Jewish Law.

Paul's 'Damascus Road' experience was a total conversion which can be interpreted in psychological terms. Conversion meant the abandonment of Paul's personal fantasy of himself as the perfect Pharisee. He was forced to accept that he could not keep the Law of God. All his boastful pride and self-respect were gone. Personal pride in the Law had been displaced by a glorying in the cross of Christ (see Galatians 6.14 and Romans 3.27). The particular emphasis is on the exclusion of pride, because here Paul's personal conflict came to its issue.

Paul's personal liberation was not complete all at once. There is evidence from his earlier letters that some of the older traits and fantasies had partly survived (see, for example, 1 Thessalonians 2.18; 1 Corinthians 4.21, 7.8–9 – counsels of perfection – 1 Corinthians 9.15; and 2 Corinthians 12.7). As Dodd sees it, Paul had not yet made that final abandonment of any claim upon life for personal and individual pride and satisfaction, which is involved in surrender to God in Christ.

Paul underwent a further spiritual crisis, of which Dodd sees the signs reflected in 2 Corinthians. The parts of the correspondence with the Corinthians are now found in the wrong order in the New Testament books. Chapters 1–9 of 2 Corinthians were written in chastened mood after the crisis which had provoked Paul to write chapters 10–13. In this crisis Paul had plumbed the spiritual depths and come to terms with the realities of his existence. His later letters demonstrate an altogether different tone and temper. In the controversies discussed in Romans and Colossians there is a new emphasis on the virtues of reconciliation. The letter to the Philippians in chapters 3–4 is held to show most clearly what this testing psychological experience had made of a naturally proud, self-assertive and impatient man (see especially 3.13–16 and 4.7–12). On the basis of this psychological reconstruction, Dodd can argue for a perceptible change of outlook in Paul's writing with regard to the future hope, the value of creation, and the universality of the Christian religion. These theological changes are correlated with the inner psychological changes witnessed in 2 Corinthians.

The biographer of C.H. Dodd, F.W. Dillistone, reveals how this interpretation of St Paul's thought was influenced directly by Dodd's own personal experience of psychotherapy:

> This experience [of a crisis in Dodd's personal life] left a deep scar and some months later he was seeking the help of Dr. J.A. Hadfield, one of the earliest practitioners in England of the new methods of psycho-analysis. Over a period of more than four years he paid periodic visits to Dr. Hadfield and . . . it is abundantly clear that at this stage of his life he became aware of the profound importance of what was then called the New Psychology, not only on account of its interpretation of the place of religion in human life but also of the possibilities which it offered for resolving in a positive way his own emotional problems . . .

And amongst the fresh developments of his own time, none seemed more valuable for the interpretation of man's endeavours and frustrations than the New Psychology with its insights into hidden repressions and the interplay of will and imagination. In particular, the conflict within the self, so vividly portrayed in the seventh chapter of the Epistle to the Romans, gains new meaning in the light of the case histories which modern psychologists have recorded. In the course of his exposition of the meaning of Paul for today Dodd drew upon the writings of the two men to whom he had turned for help with his own problems – J.A. Hadfield and Fearon Halliday.

(Dillistone, 1977, pp. 79, 89)

Although such immediate and personal experience can transform a reading and inspire a new interpretation, it may be too close and dominant, so that it overwhelms a more balanced view. The results are too highly charged and personal, when they should be more reflective and theological. It is the danger inherent in any comparative study that the connections one can see straight away become the whole answer.

Chapter 8

Allegory or spiritual reading

In the long history of Christian interpretation of the Bible, the ancient practice of allegory is probably the most widely used and consistently chosen method of interpretative reading. Nowadays, by contrast, allegory is frequently condemned and dismissed, for several reasons. It is seen as an unscholarly and unethical way to treat a text, essentially by reading into the text the meaning which you wish subsequently to read out of, and derive from, that text. Secondly it appears to be an arbitrary practice, dependent upon the whim or enthusiasm of the reader, and lacking in effective controls or means of assessment. And finally, many Christians now regard allegory as less true to their faith than the comparably long-standing method of typology.

Before we go any further, it is necessary to define these terms and to illustrate the difference between allegory and typology. If we investigate the root idea of the word, we discover that 'allegory' as a principle of interpretation treats the text as having an indirect or less than straightforward meaning; according to Heraclitus (talking of the meaning of the epic poems of Homer) it is 'speaking one thing and signifying *something other than what is said*'. While allegory claims that the real meaning of the text has practically no continuity with the historical situation of the original author and his surface meaning, typology argues for a real continuity of meaning across the spectrum of the biblical texts. As part of the overall theological plan, which is perceived to embrace both Old and New Testaments, an event or personality within the Old Testament corresponds to, and prefigures, a character or happening in the New Testament story. So, while the opportunities for allegory are open-ended and uncontrolled, the process of typology is closed (and apparently confirmed) by the recognition of a correspondence in biblical theology.

The original impulse for such methods of interpretation resembles problem-solving. In an extreme case, Sir William Drummond in the early nineteenth century attempted to prove that many parts of the Old Testament were allegories, chiefly derived from astronomy (his *Oedipus Judaicus* was first published in 1811). More reasonably, it is possible to ease the difficulty of a puzzling text, or reconcile divergent manuscripts, and produce an innocuous or even an edifying interpretation by such means. The Church Father Origen (*c.*185–*c.*253 CE) is often regarded as the authority on allegory. He certainly represents the Alexandrian tradition of biblical interpretation at its most elaborate; he showed the potential of allegory not only in practice but also in methodological theory. But Origen did not invent the method. He inherited it from his predecessor Clement and before him the Jewish expositor Philo (*c.*20 BCE–50 CE), all associated with Alexandria.

Philo sought to represent the vitality of Jewish theology and ethics in terms of Greek philosophy, thus solving the problems that Hellenistic thinkers might experience with such alien concepts. For example, he writes about the Jewish pilgrimage to the Holy Land: 'Entrance into the land is entrance into philosophy. This is the good and fertile land which bears fruit, which produces the divine plants, the virtues' (*Q.E.* 2.13). The migration of Abraham, the father of the Jews, to the promised land, is an allegory of a human soul that loves virtue wandering in search of the true God (*Abr.* 68).

The technique of allegory can be traced back yet further, to Greek interpreters of Homeric poetry as early as the sixth century BCE. The negative justification for such interpretations, against the background of traditional Greek religion, was to defend such poetry, telling of the exploits of the deities of Olympus, from charges of immorality and blasphemy. More positively, the aim was to unearth deeper meanings and underlying senses: such stories, it was said, are really about human psychology and moral truths.

Perhaps, given its pedigree, we should not automatically exclude allegory from consideration. It actually forms part of the historical otherness of the biblical text; that sense of historical difference warrants the reader's respect, if the text is not to be treated unethically. Further, the individual creativity of the allegorical interpretation, often criticised as arbitrariness, should be seen to reflect, in its own way, the modern concern for the reader to be taken up into the text, participate in it, and interact with its meaning. Modern literary readings look at structures, whether surface or deep structures, and so analyse the patterns and relationships within the text. Such methods can set up thematic arrangements which are very reminiscent of those allegorical interpretations in the past. In addition it is possible that allegory may be assessed, if not constrained, by the critical scrutiny of such thematic patterns.

First we need to substantiate the fact that allegory belongs within the New Testament, and not just in its interpretation. We should also examine briefly how the method was expounded subsequently by the Church Fathers. In the Gospels there is one important story (parable) attributed to Jesus which is explicitly presented as an allegory. This is the story of the vineyard tenants in Mark 12.1–12:

> A man planted a vineyard, put a fence around it, dug a pit for the wine press, and built a watchtower; then he leased it to tenants and went to another country. When the season came, he sent a slave to the tenants to collect from them his share of the produce of the vineyard. But they seized him, and beat him, and sent him away empty-handed. And again he sent another slave to them; this one they beat over the head and insulted. Then he sent another, and that one they killed. And so it was with many others; some they beat, and others they killed. He had still one other, a beloved son. Finally he sent him to them, saying, 'They will respect my son.' But those tenants said to one another, 'This is the heir; come, let us kill him, and the inheritance will be ours.' So they seized him, killed him, and threw him out of the vineyard. What then will the owner of the vineyard do? He will come and destroy the tenants and give the vineyard to others. Have you not read this Scripture:
>
>> 'The stone that the builders rejected has become the cornerstone; this was the Lord's doing, and it is amazing in our eyes' ?
>
> When they [the chief priests, scribes and elders] realized that he had told this parable against them, they wanted to arrest him, but they feared the crowd. So they left him and went away.

The allegorical elements are intrinsic to this story, and it seems to be made to point prophetically to Jesus' own death. The owner is God, the beloved son is Jesus, the vineyard (as in Isaiah 5) is Israel, the tenants are the Jewish leaders, and the slaves are the Old Testament prophets. This is no simple story of agricultural malpractice, but the conclusion both makes the application clear and confirms the correspondences that are to be drawn with the religious world. Other elements in the story, such as fence, pit, wine press and watchtower, do not seem to have direct allegorical equivalents. They are part of the story's realistic colouring; some readers would say that they are evidence of a natural story that has evolved into a religious allegory.

Certainly many other allegories evolved in the later interpretations of other Gospel parables attributed, in their original form, to Jesus. A good example is the interpretation of the parable of the sower, in Mark 4.14–20 and parallels, where the secondary character of the interpretation compared with the original story is fairly apparent. The allegorical method of interpretation was especially common later among both Greek and Latin fathers of the Christian Church in the Patristic period. A striking example is this exposition of the parable of the Good Samaritan (Luke 10.29–37) at the start of a homily by Severus of Antioch (d. 538 CE):

> *A certain man was going down from Jerusalem to Jericho.* The use of the specific noun is to the point: not 'somebody was going down' but 'a certain man'; for the whole of humanity is in question, inasmuch as it has fallen, through the disobedience of Adam, from the height of the abode of Paradise – lofty and calm, passionless and godlike, here aptly called 'Jerusalem', which means 'peace of God' – to the depth of Jericho, low-lying and stifled in heat – meaning the ardent life of this world, which separates from God and drags down, which causes suffocation in the heat of shameful desire, and chokes to death. Once humanity had gone astray towards this life, and had lost her balance and been drawn down, borne little by little to the lowest point of the downward path, as I have said, there settled on her a swarm of savage demons, like a band of brigands; and they stripped her of the cloak of virtue, leaving her not a vestige of fortitude or temperance or justice or prudence, or of anything that represented the image of God; and so they hacked her to death with the repeated wounds of various sins, leaving her cut to pieces; in a word half-dead.
>
> So while humanity was lying prostrate and all but fainting to death, she was visited by the Mosaic Law; for this is, of course, the meaning of the priest and levite, since it was the Law that taught the levitic priesthood. It did indeed visit her, but it fell

short in competence, and was not equal to a full treatment; it did not even raise the prostrate form, but went perforce, in its incompetence, on an ineffectual round. For sacrifices and gifts were offered through it, as Paul said, which were unable to perfect the worshipper in conscience; because, again, it was impossible that the blood of bulls and goats should entirely take away sin. . . . At last *a certain Samaritan who was on a journey came to where he was.*

According to Severus's reading the parable has become an allegory of what has happened to humanity from Adam to Christ (to whom, of course, the Samaritan corresponds). The story ends with a communal understanding of the preacher and his hearers, as the representatives of humanity at that day. The inn, where the story closes for the time being, is referred to by a Greek word which means literally 'all-receiving'. The inn is the Church which exists for all people, and the two coins are the talents which the members of the Church must spend among people. The activity of the Church is advocated, as essentially useful, until such time as the Samaritan (Christ) returns, as he promises he will. The moral for the Christian Church is that it must remain open and Christ-centred until the world ends.

Severus's homily is a highly developed, rather extreme, example. But it should not be concluded that allegory only has a place in the Christian tradition well after the New Testament period. There is enough evidence, apart from the parable of the vineyard tenants, to demonstrate a gradual but natural evolution of this interpretative method from within the Bible itself. Paul uses a complicated allegory in Galatians 4.21–5.1 where (as he admits) he allegorises the history of Israel, in order to bring out a clearly polarised statement of theology:

Tell me, you who desire to be subject to the law, will you not listen to the law? For it is written that Abraham had two sons, one by a slave woman and the other by a free woman. One, the child of the slave, was born according to the flesh; the other, the child of the free woman, was born through the promise. Now this is an allegory: these women are two covenants. One woman, in fact, is Hagar, from Mount Sinai, bearing children for slavery. Now Hagar is Mount Sinai in Arabia and corresponds to the present Jerusalem, for she is in slavery with her children. But the other woman corresponds to the Jerusalem above; she is free, and she is our mother. For it is written,

> Rejoice, you childless one, you who bear no children,
> burst into song and shout, you who endure no birthpangs;
> for the children of the desolate woman are more numerous
> than the children of the one who is married.

Now you, my friends, are children of the promise, like Isaac. But just as at that time the child who was born according to the flesh persecuted the child who was born according to the Spirit, so it is now also. But what does the Scripture say? 'Drive out the slave and her child; for the child of the slave will not share the inheritance with the child of the free woman.' So then, friends, we are children, not of the slave but of the free woman. For freedom Christ has set us free. Stand firm, therefore, and do not submit again to a yoke of slavery.

Elsewhere in Paul's writing, the treatment of the balance and contrast between the first and the second (or last) figures of Adam, in 1 Corinthians 15.21–2, 45–50 and in Romans 5.12–21, is more strictly an example of typology (see Romans 5.14). But in 1 Corinthians 9.9–12 the literal meaning of the ancient law of Deuteronomy 25.4 is denied, in favour of a much broader allegorical/spiritual interpretation:

> For it is written in the law of Moses, 'You shall not muzzle an ox while it is treading out the grain.' Is it for oxen that God is concerned? Or does he not speak entirely for our sake? It was indeed written for our sake, for whoever ploughs should plough in hope and whoever threshes should thresh in hope of a share in the crop. If we have sown spiritual good among you, is it too much if we reap your material benefits? If others share this rightful claim on you, do not we still more?

In the fourth Gospel also the larger meaning is asserted, when it is declared that the whole meaning of the Old Testament is Jesus Christ: Jesus said 'You search the Scriptures because you think that in them you have eternal life; and it is they that testify on my behalf' (John 5.39). In his commentary on John's Gospel, the Church Father Origen seems to be taking this text as a key to unlock the whole Bible, applying it to the fourth Gospel as well, and using it to lift up and allegorise what might have appeared to be literal expressions:

We have now to transform the Gospel known to sense-perception into one intellectual and spiritual. For what would the narrative of the Gospel known to sense-perception amount to, if it were not developed into a spiritual one? It would be of little account or none. Anyone can read it and assure himself of the facts it tells – nothing more. But our whole energy is now to be directed to the effort to penetrate to the depths of the meaning of the Gospel and to search out the truth that is in it when it is divested of its prefigurations.

(Commentary 1.10)

There are few theologians who have known the Bible as well as Origen did. He was able to draw in the full range of scriptural texts to demonstrate his argument, to illuminate the meaning of another text, or to solve problems. The totality of Scripture, represented by the Greek Bible, was in Origen's belief inspired by the Holy Spirit; this was true down to the last dot, and the inspiration also covered alternative readings in the text. But it was not simply to be read literally. 'Spiritual truth can be preserved in material falsehood.' And differing, if apparently factual accounts, may be designed by God to provide a range of spiritual meanings.

The hidden meaning is of primary importance. God's revelation has been accommodated to the human capacity for under-standing. To put it negatively, God does not cast pearls before swine, not only for the sake of the pearls, but also to preserve the swine from blaspheming in ignorance. Again, to put it positively, one could say that God starts from where we are: Scripture is provided as part of an educational process for humanity. We would not be able to absorb the full truth all at once. Students apparently value more highly the knowledge for which they have had to dig more deeply. So the Bible provides the stages in a process towards deeper truths.

As well as writing commentaries and preaching sermons, Origen set out the theoretical principles by which he believed biblical interpretation should operate. He distinguished three basic levels of meaning in Scripture: the literal, the moral/edificatory, and the spiritual/mystical. This formal structure of three levels was explained on analogy with human psychology, where it corresponded to the body, the soul and the spirit respectively in a human being. To support this idea, Origen used a scriptural proof-text which he found in the Septuagint Greek version of Proverbs 22.20. This translates as 'Describe these things in a threefold way' – clearly the Greek differs from the text underlying modern English versions.

Another biblical text appeared to Origen to justify limiting the number of levels of meaning, perhaps by concentrating on two. This text was John 2.6, from the story of the wedding at Cana: 'And there were set there six waterpots of stone, after the manner of the purifying of the Jews, containing *two or three* firkins apiece.' But to use this option, and to reduce the number of meanings to two rather than three, would only mean for Origen a discounting of the text's literal meaning. In practice Origen rarely elaborated all three levels of meaning at once. His tract *On Pascha* is in fact an exception, because here the first two levels of meaning are found running together, with the spiritual exegesis of the same text in a separate section at the end.

It is not always easy to sustain a clear distinction, even in Origen's own work, between the moral/edificatory and the spiritual/mystical senses. Sometimes Origen distinguished them as differing levels of spiritual attainment in a progression towards Christian maturity. Elsewhere the distinction may be more one of content than of exegetical method, for 'the spiritual interpretation is that which relates to Christ and the great truths of God's saving dispensation, whereas the moral interpretation is one which relates to human experience'. Such distinctions in content can of course be elaborated with the development of new interpretations. The variety in the level of spiritual meanings which Origen himself offered can be classified as christological (to do with Christ), ecclesiological (concerning the Church), mystical, and eschatological (about the future and the last things). Such classifications were in fact used to the full in later systems of exegesis.

A straightforward example might be helpful at this point. When the Bible refers to the place-name Jerusalem, then the literal meaning is obviously that of the city in Judah, King David's capital city. At the moral level of meaning the reference is to the faithful Christian soul. The spiritual meaning is the Church of Christ. And we must not forget the eschatological meaning, seen in the New Testament itself, where the new Jerusalem is the heavenly city.

It has already been observed that a powerful motive for allegorical explanations was problem-solving. Origen was convinced that Scripture contained 'thousands of instances, recorded as actual events, but which did not happen literally' – they are 'not true, but actually absurd and impossible'. Many of the instances come from the Old Testament, but

> even the Gospels are full of passages of this kind, as when the devil takes Jesus up into a *high mountain* in order to show him from thence *the kingdoms of the whole world and the glory of them*. [Matthew 4.8] For what man who does not read such passages carelessly would fail to condemn those who believe that with the eye of the flesh, which requires a great height to enable us to perceive what is below and at our feet, the kingdoms of the Persians, Scythians, Indians and Parthians were seen, and the manner in which their rulers are glorified by men? And the careful reader will detect thousands of other passages like this in the Gospels, which will convince him that events which did not take place at all are woven into the records of what literally did happen.

Such an attitude might savour of modern rationalism or scepticism. But the imaginative, or inspirational, solutions which Origen produced for these problems would never satisfy these modern critics. Instead of discarding or explaining away such texts, Origen raised them to new levels of meaning and justified them as divine revelation. These texts could be revelatory for later generations of hearers or readers, rather than standing or falling on the grounds of historical plausibility for the writer's original situation.

In recent years there has been a dramatic change in critical presuppositions, reacting against the modernist historicism that has held centre stage since the Enlightenment. The effect is to bring the modern reader potentially much closer to Origen's practice of allegory, and more sympathetic to his intentions. As Frances Young described the modern context:

> the books of Scripture are not simply historical documents permitting access to revelatory events behind the text to which the texts give testimony. For it is only the way the story is told in the biblical material that makes the events significant in any sense. That means we are dealing with literature, and response to story, no matter how 'history-like', involves dimensions other than a documentary reading.

> Readers are invited to read themselves into texts, and allegory might be regarded as one way of making a text mean something meaningful to the reader. There is no responsibility to the

illusory 'original meaning' or to the absent author. There is therefore no dishonesty in allegory after all.

(1993, pp. 105, 108)

We need to look afresh at the possibilities of allegorical reading. A book by Jon Whitman (1987) on the dynamics of allegory can assist in this:

> Our language is constantly telling us that something is what it is not. . . . All fiction . . . tries to express a truth by departing from it in some way. It may embellish its subject, rearrange it, or simply verbalize it, but in every case, that ancient dislocation of words from their objects will keep the language at one remove from what it claims to present. Allegory is the extreme case of this divergence. . . . In its obliquity, allegorical writing thus exposes in an extreme way the foundation of fiction in general.
>
> The more allegory exploits the divergence between corresponding levels of meaning, the less tenable the correspondence becomes. Alternatively, the more it closes ranks and emphasizes the correspondence, the less oblique, and therefore the less allegorical, the divergence becomes.
>
> (1987, pp. 1–2)

When there are dramatic changes of cultural context, allegory can function in a liberating way, to develop ideological readings. Essentially it is saying, 'You have read the text that way, but it should be read like this.' One can see the fruits of this process in the radically different readings of liberation theology (in its many forms) and in feminist theologies.

To quote Frances Young again:

> The theological task is in principle infinite and beyond human capacity. Scripture itself provides paradigms of pilgrimage, of progress and set-back, of faith and hope, rather than concepts, doctrines or definitions. Furthermore the texts themselves point forwards, referring not just to events of the past, or to present experience, but to the future, often a visionary future guaranteed by partial anticipation in present experience, known by faith not sight. And that future, we are promised, is one of 'performance', of playing harps, of worship.
>
> (1990, p. 182)

How would such participation in, and interaction with, the text work out in practice? Frances Young (one of the few to explore this area) writes in terms of imitation and performance, seeing the value of the text as an icon for moral behaviour and a symbol for theological ideas.

As a practical example, one could consider this passage. It impinges on the New Testament symbol of the Last Judgement, and it could be regarded as a kind of interpretative commentary in reverse on the traditions of Matthew's Gospel (especially 25.31–46 and 28.16–20). At heart it functions as an allegory:

At the end of time, billions of people were scattered on a great plain before God's throne. Most shrank back from the brilliant light before them. But some groups near the front talked heatedly – not with cringing shame, but with belligerence.

'Can God judge us? How can he know about suffering?' snapped a pert young brunette. She ripped open a sleeve to reveal a tattooed number from a Nazi concentration camp. 'We endured terror . . . beatings . . . torture . . . death!' In another group a negro boy lowered his collar. 'What about this?' he demanded, showing an ugly rope burn. 'Lynched for no crime but being black!' In another crowd, a pregnant schoolgirl with sullen eyes. 'Why should I suffer?' she murmured. 'It wasn't my fault.'

Far out across the plain were hundreds of such groups. Each had a complaint against God for the evil and suffering permitted in his world. How lucky God was to live in heaven where all was sweetness and light, where there was no weeping or fear, no hunger nor hatred. What did God know of all that men had been forced to endure in this world? For God lives a pretty sheltered life, they said.

So each of these groups sent forth their leader, chosen because he had suffered the most. A Jew, a negro, a person from Hiroshima, a horribly deformed arthritic, a thalidomide child. In the centre of the plain they consulted with each other. At last they were ready to present their case. It was rather clever.

Before God could be qualified to be their judge, he must endure what they endured. Their decision was that God should be sentenced to live on earth – as a man! Let him be born a Jew. Let the legitimacy of his birth be doubted! Give him a work so difficult that even his family will think him out of his mind when he tries to do it. Let him be betrayed by his closest friends. Let him face false charges, be tried by a prejudiced jury and convicted by a cowardly judge. Let him be tortured. At the last, let him see what it is to be terribly alone. Then let him die. Let him die so there can be no doubt he died. Let there be a great host of witnesses to verify it.

As each leader announced his portion of the sentence, loud murmurs of approval went up from the throng of people assembled. When the last had finished pronouncing sentence there was a long silence. No-one uttered another word. No-one moved. For suddenly all knew that *God had already served his sentence*.

A further practical example has its focus more directly in Matthew 25.31–46. This is a fairly modern dramatised version of the parable of the sheep and the goats; by its allegorical application it has moved the meaning of the parable a long way from Matthew's original intentions (but may be none the worse for that):

Matthew 25 – The Final Exam

The curtain opens, and JC (wearing his best jeans) is seen in the middle of a huge crowd divided into 2 groups. He begins speaking to one of the groups (left or right, depends which side you're looking from).

– You people didn't know how to live, did you?
It seems you didn't live out your lives in the way you were meant to. You were surrounded by death and poverty, and you went through life as if you didn't see anything yourselves.
JC starts pointing at individuals

– One day I came to borrow a pint of milk and a loaf of bread and *you* told me you didn't believe in borrowing and lending. I lived next door to you, and you didn't want to know.

– Another day *you* in the pin-stripe suit gossiped about my clothes: 'Looks as if he buys them at the Oxfam shop' you said. You forgot I'd been made redundant and was living off Social Security.

– I finished my days in a geriatric nursing home, and *you* in the blue skirt were my daughter, and it obviously pained you to visit me for half-an-hour a fortnight. I'd brought you into the world and you made me feel useless and a nuisance!

At that point one of the accused interrupted:

– I think *you've* made a mistake, sir. With all respect to yourself and no harm intended, I never once saw you in all my life.

– He's right *(said someone else)*; you never lived in our town. *Then JC answered (well you know what he answered)*:

– Don't you realise that, while there was just one ill or lonely person in your town, I couldn't be healthy or happy?

– You with the white trousers, you so easily switched off the 'Appeal for the Week' and opened a second bottle of whisky, without asking yourself whether you could help.

– You over there in the corner, you used to laugh at the 'do-gooders' in your town, but you were a 'do-nothing' yourself.

– You in the green pullover, you were always shouting for longer and stricter prison sentences, but you never once entered a prison to see what it was like, nor did you ever see or visit a prisoner.

And now JC looks at the other group. He immediately relaxes, looks at them with great affection, even lights up a cigarette (Govt. Health Warning: Smoking Can Seriously Endanger Your Life) in his excitement and happiness. He talks with them . . .

Hello my buddies, bosom pals, sweethearts . . . it's lovely to see you all. You are as welcome as the flowers in May, and I hope you'll all stay around for a long, long time . . . There's no lack of beds or food or drink. When I was with you, you treated me well, like a king in fact.

Then one of his listeners jumps to his feet and challenges JC:

– Excuse me correcting you, sir, but I believe you must be thinking of another group of people. None of us ever knew you. *(Then JC answers the man . . . well you know what he answered)*

– You're the one who is mistaken, my lad. Because every time you did something for people worse off than yourself you were really doing it for me. I was there all the time.

(But now a convinced atheist jumps to his feet)

– At least *I'm* an exception to that, sir. I always did things for my fellow human-beings. I never believed in God or religion. *(Those near him try to make him sit down)*

– Be quiet, you'll lose heaven saying things like that!

But JC answers him:

– Well now, your intellectual pride has burst like a balloon, my son. It was always your principal fault, but you made up for it by the way you looked after me in the poor, the political prisoners, and all the rest. Welcome home!

Background music begins to swell, perhaps Beethoven's Ninth Symphony, on one side, and teeth-gnashing sounds on the other. Just before the curtains close, God the Father goes up to the teeth-gnashers and says to them:

– I couldn't bear to think of you all roasting in the fires of hell. I'll see you all again when I've finished looking at 'Coronation Street'.

And now the curtains really do close, and you can read on them:
'THE END'

And in small print: 'Any resemblance to real-life persons is completely and entirely intentional'.

Chapter 9

Texts as slogans

Just as the characters of script are dead, lacking a life of their own, begetting neither joy nor sorrow until they meet and touch, so it is with people, or with dogs or the books of the Koran, or grapes upon the vine.

David Grossman, *The Smile of the Lamb*

An important primary question still to be asked concerns the function of a New Testament text, that is to say the range of functions which it may still possess, within those generations after the one in which the text may be said to have originated. This question often has its sharpest focus when it is asked about an extract from the text, a chapter or maybe even a verse, used in isolation. One should ask about the purpose of quotation, the applications to which the text is put, and the methods by which it is used.

To give an example: are what may be called partisan applications, such as those which require devotional functions of the text in the liturgy of the Church, or kerygmatic functions in its teaching and preaching, or even dogmatic functions in the evolution of Christian doctrine from the Bible, to be seen as in a totally different category from all other uses of the Bible, all other readings of the New Testament, that happen outside of the Churches? Certainly even within the Church there would be a variety of responses to this primary question from the different denominations of Christians. So even there the practice is by no means uniform.

Some of the implications of these questions will become clearer if we look at a range of historical examples. In many different periods Christians have chosen selections of short quotations from the Bible and set these up in their Churches; here they may function as aids to meditation, as summaries of fundamental truths for teaching purposes, or as slogans for use in missionary evangelism, perhaps provoking a controversial response (rather like the 'wayside pulpit' posters outside Churches in more modern times).

> At that time [just after the General Strike] it was a common practice for chapels and churches to have on a notice board outside the building what was called 'The Wayside Pulpit', a text or a slogan that was changed each week. I always found them distasteful and had got into the habit of averting my eyes when passing them, in order to prevent myself from losing my temper. But one I could not ignore, because Phil, who was an undergraduate at the time, with an equally hot-headed friend, tore it down in anger. It read: 'A drop in a man's wages is bad enough, but a drop too much is worse.' The minister and the deacons were very cross with the boys and threatened to suspend them from church membership, whereupon I felt compelled to write to the minister in support of them, saying that I hoped that, had I been their age, I would have had the pluck to treat so mean a message as they had done.
>
> (Walter Allen, *All in a Lifetime*, p. 154)

Of the Church of St Mary the Virgin at Elham, south of Canterbury, John Betjeman wrote: 'To many this is the most beautiful parish Church in Kent.' One of its most interesting features is an eighteenth-century set of text-boards, hanging between the arches high up on either side of the nave. They were provided at the expense of the Churchwardens in 1760. The choice of scriptural texts clearly reflects the concern of that period for upright ethical living as the essence of religion.

On the south side these texts are:

> He hath shewed thee, O man, what is good; and what doth the Lord require of thee, but to do justly, and to love mercy, and to walk humbly with thy God.
>
> (Micah 6.8)

> Beloved, follow not that which is evil, but that which is good. He that doeth good is of God; but he that doeth evil hath not seen God.
>
> (3 John 11)

Let all bitterness, and wrath, and anger, and clamour, and evil speaking, be put away from you, with all malice.

(Ephesians 4.31)

God is a Spirit; and they that worship him must worship him in spirit and in truth.

(John 4.24)

On the north side are the following:

Keep thy foot when thou goest to the house of God, and be more ready to hear, than to give the sacrifice of fools; for they consider not that they do evil.

(Ecclesiastes 5.1)

Let us walk honestly, as in the day; not in rioting and drunkenness, not in chambering or wantonness, not in strife and envying.

(Romans 13.13)

If ye will not hear, and if ye will not lay it to heart, to give glory unto my name, saith the Lord of Hosts, I will even send a curse upon you, and I will curse your blessings.

(Malachi 2.2)

Thou shalt open my lips, O Lord: and my mouth shall shew thy praise.

(Psalm 51.15)

Seven out of the eight quotations are from the Authorised Version, while the eighth and last is from the 1535 translation of the Psalms by Miles Coverdale.

Nearly eighty years earlier, a series of texts in the form of wall-paintings was executed at the Church of St John the Baptist at Stokesay, next to Stokesay Castle, between Ludlow and Shrewsbury, in Shropshire. The work cost £6.12s in 1683. Mr Thomas Francis painted the texts 'within somewhat coarsely baroque architectural surrounds', according to David C. George in the Church guidebook.

These are the texts that were selected, reading on the north side of the Church, starting from the east end. First, the Sermon on the Mount text, now defaced:

treasures on earth . . . lay up for yourselves treasures in heaven where neither moth nor rust.

(Matthew 6.19f)

And when ye stand praying, forgive if ye have aught against any, that your Father who is in heaven may forgive.

(Mark 11.25)

This is accompanied by the Lord's Prayer, now covered by a monument. Then there are the Ten Commandments (Exodus 20) in two sections, flanked by the figures of Moses and Aaron. Then:

Blessed be the Lord God of our fathers which hath put such a thing as this in ye King's heart to beautify ye house.

(Ezra 7.27)

On the west wall are the fragmentary remains of a text which was concerned with the healing miracles, including the words 'brought', 'children unto', 'touch' (Matthew 19.13?).

The following texts are painted on the south side of the Church (reading from the east end):

Come eat of my bread and drink of the wine which I have mingled . . . forsake ye food . . .

(Proverbs 9.5)

As newborn babes desire ye sincere milk of ye word that ye may grow thereby.

(1 Peter 2.2 – found by the pulpit)

This is followed by the Apostles' Creed, together with the benefactions record of Roger Powell (1616). Then:

Keep thy foot when thou goest to the house of God, and be more ready to hear than to give ye sacrifice of fools.

(Ecclesiastes 5.1)

'How dreadful is this place. This is none other but the House of God, and this is ye gate of heaven.

(Genesis 28.17)

One thing have I desired of the Lord all . . . I may . . . house of the Lord . . . all life to behold ye . . . Lord to enquire . . .

(Psalm 27.4)

Many of the wall-paintings have been obscured wholly or partially by funerary monuments, some with nineteenth-century dates. This presumably indicates the different order of priorities of a later age, although it is possible that the paintings had become lost to sight in the last century, rather than being deliberately defaced. These paintings have recently been restored with aid from the Canterbury Cathedral Wallpaintings Workshop.

A much more recent example – in fact almost 280 years later – is provided by the eight Tablets of the Word in the nave of Coventry Cathedral. This modern cathedral, designed by Sir Basil Spence, was consecrated in May 1962. The Tablets of the Word are the work of a sculptor, Ralph Beyer, whose father Oskar Beyer was an authority on the incised lettering and symbols in the Roman catacombs. The tablets are blocks of white Hollington stone measuring 15 feet by 6 feet, placed six feet off the ground in the window recesses of the nave, to benefit from the side-lighting. The texts with appropriate accompanying symbols are carved in beautiful yet uneven letters, perhaps to emphasise that they are carved by a person not a machine; they may also imply the 'primitive' origins of the sayings.

The principle of selection of these texts was to 'present important aspects of Christian teaching and be a mirror of the Life of our Lord' (Basil Spence, *Phoenix at Coventry*, 1962, p. 75). It can be noticed that certain liberties are taken in combining texts from different sources, just as in a meditative manner when quotations are linked from memory. This is the sequence of texts at Coventry:

1 'I and the Father are One. He that hath seen me hath seen the Father' (John 10.30; 14.9). Symbols: the sun and the chi-rho.
2 'The Son of Man is come to seek and to save that which is lost. The good shepherd giveth his life for the sheep' (Luke 19.10; John 10.11). Symbols: the good shepherd and a cross.
3 'Come unto me all ye that labour and are heavy laden and I will give you rest. Take my yoke upon you and learn of me, for I am meek and lowly in heart, and ye shall find rest unto your souls' (Matthew 11.28f). Symbol: the cross.
4 'A new commandment I give unto you, that ye love one another as I have loved you' (John 13.34). Symbol: two hands showing wounds.
5 'I am the vine; ye are the branches. He that abideth in me and I in

him the same beareth much fruit, for apart from me ye can do
nothing' (John 15.5). Symbol: the grapevine.

6 'When the Comforter is come, whom I will send unto you from
the Father, even the Spirit of Truth, which proceedeth from the
Father, he shall testify of me; and ye also shall bear witness'
(John 15.26f). No symbol.

7 'Whoso eateth my flesh and drinketh my blood hath eternal life'
(John 6.54). Symbols: loaf and chalice.

8 'Fear not, I am the first and the last. I am alive for evermore,
amen; and have the keys of hell and of death' (Revelation 1.17f).
Symbol: key.

There are three other striking examples of the explicit use of
biblical texts in the design of Coventry Cathedral. At the east end of
the bombed cathedral ruins, behind the charred cross made from
fifteenth-century roof-beams, is found the direct and simple prayer
'Father Forgive' (Luke 23.34). The inscription, carved by appren-
tices of Coventry Technical College, in the stone base of the altar in
the Chapel of Christ the Servant (the Industrial Chaplaincy centre)
reads 'I am among you as one that serves' (Luke 22.27). And finally
the text from Haggai 2.9, used by Archbishop Michael Ramsey in his
sermon at the consecration of the cathedral, is engraved beneath
the spire: 'The latter glory of this house shall be greater than the
former, saith the Lord of Hosts, and in this place I will give peace.'

As with the Tablets of the Word in Coventry Cathedral, the way
the Bible is used is not only by explicit citations of the text. There
can also be implicit echoes of the text in the use of biblical symbols;
these function as reminders of the associated texts. In the same way
to identify a biblical character may recall the whole story associated
with that person in the New (or Old) Testaments. The particular
technique known as 'typology' uses this recollection to special
effect (see chapter 8). A positive relationship is created between
two figures, one from the New Testament has its prototype in
another from the Old Testament. The whole biblical story of the
one person merges into what is being said theologically about her
or his counterpart.

One of the oldest and most spectacular exemplifications of this
symbolic/typological use of the Bible is in the windows of stained
glass and in the carved statues of the doorways of Chartres
Cathedral. The whole medieval building then becomes a total
biblical symbol in itself. Not only are there the triumphant entrances

which celebrate the glory of Jesus and of his mother; there is also a counterbalance of prophecy and fulfilment between the north and south sides of the building. On the one side are the prophets and the prototypes of the Messiah: Balaam, Isaiah, Jeremiah, Simeon, John the Baptist, Melchizedek, Abraham, Moses, Samuel and David. On the other side are the apostles, evangelists and fathers of the Church: Matthew, Philip, Thomas, Andrew and Peter, Theodore, Stephen, Clement and Laurence.

This set of examples, both ancient and more modern, both explicit and implicit, already shows how wide is the range of use of the Bible within the Christian tradition. But they are only examples, to encourage a more active recognition of the variety of possibilities. It is of course important that all such examples should be studied in their particular contexts, to ask why certain texts or symbols were selected at that particular time, and what factors may have influenced the decisions. One can also see the pervasive effect of some biblical themes and traditions which recur so often over the centuries within the quotations and the iconography.

Our current progression through ways of reading the New Testament, of handling these texts and interacting with them, is almost at an end. But the virtue (if it is one) of the modern pluralism of approaches, and relativity of outlook, is that one never reaches the ultimate conclusion. There may always be fresh combinations of ideas, and insights from a new angle on a text, just around the corner. Possibilities for exploration seem almost infinite, not only beyond the present frontiers, but also in efforts to understand how earlier generations related to their chosen texts.

Because of the extensive use made of methods from secular sources, in order to study these religious texts, it is easy to slip into a relaxed approach whereby the New Testament is literature, just like other literatures. This is by no means a negative outlook and may prove beneficial. But, as we have noticed several times on our journey, these texts (like exceptional texts of literature) retain the power to engage and involve the reader, challenging and provoking an extraordinary degree of interaction. The power of the short text as an effective slogan might symbolise this effect for us. Just as the first Christians (to the best of our knowledge) seem to have responded to Christ and acknowledged him with a slogan, or acclamation-formula, such as 'Jesus is Lord', so later generations, reading the New Testament, have sought to summarise their faith and religious insights by a compelling choice of quotations.

Perhaps the modern reader, from literary perspectives, may still recognise the quotation as a most effective means of response to such texts. To adopt some words of Jacques Ellul,

> western society shows itself very destructive of worn-out symbols and yet an avid consumer of living symbols which link this new world to the deepest roots of one's being and which restore the sacred to its imperial position.
>
> (1975, p. 70)

Chapter 10

Reading in action: John 21

It is now high time for practicalities, so we shall present a working example, based on the text of John 21. This is intended as an exercise in which you are invited to participate from the start. The aim is to demonstrate the underlying methods and the wide scope of interpretive possibilities presently available when reading a text from the New Testament. Of course the particular interest in the New Testament is but one instance of a general issue which concerns the reading of any ancient text, or indeed of any text which has an identifiable tradition behind it.

Our particular example is selected for several reasons. It is quite short and self-contained; although chapter 21 seems to function as an epilogue to the fourth Gospel, it has the features of an apocryphal fragment with a separate existence. Many readers may be familiar with the basic story already; the novelty consists in recognising that there are a multitude of ways of understanding it.

GENERAL APPROACH

The conventions of modern biblical criticism are founded on a set of assumptions about the correct way to prepare the ground for understanding a selected text. We should follow this method if we agree that, in order to understand a text properly today, we need to take account of how the text might have been understood when it was first written. Many modern readers wish to short-circuit this process, for a variety of reasons which we must take seriously. Essentially they say it is the modern interaction of a text with its readers that matters, and everything else is irrelevant or only of antiquarian interest.

Important though this attitude is, I think that if we are going to study a text thoroughly it is necessary to know something about the historical issues as well. Once we have this awareness, we can make an informed decision about each stage in the process, as to how useful or useless it may be for our reading of the text. Some stages – such as the first two that will be described – may be more relevant than we thought. Indeed we might find ourselves having to take them on trust, as the results of scholarship, simply because they are so indispensable.

STAGE 1: THE RELIABILITY OF THE ORIGINAL WORDING OF THE TEXT

John 21 is written in the form of the ancient Greek language known as New Testament Greek. Naturally there are differences of vocabulary and style between the writers of the New Testament, but they have in common a basis in the popular/colloquial Greek, known as *Koine* (or Common), which was an international language used for speaking and writing in the Mediterranean world. What they wrote was a kind of Hellenistic Jewish Greek, that could be described as a subcategory of *Koine* Greek. The Greek language basis used by the New Testament writers might also be called 'biblical' Greek because it is influenced by familiarity, in Jewish and Christian religious circles, with translations of the Hebrew Bible (the Old Testament) into Greek. This 'translation Greek' has been coloured by the Semitic phrases and biblical imagery it was seeking to convey.

So the conclusion is that the language is frequently quite colloquial, but may also have religious resonances. Most of us need to take on trust what the linguists say about the character of the language in which our text was first written. It is important because it is obvious that the language vehicle used may have influenced the historic meaning of the text.

A further point is our need of reassurance that the original wording of our text is reliable. Or we need to have pointed out to us those parts that are disputed. Here we are in the hands of the textual critics. Some have raised questions about the whole unit, the entire chapter 21. No modern scholar has campaigned more fervently than R. Alan Culpepper that John's Gospel should be studied 'as it stands rather than its sources, historical background, or themes'. But even he argues that John 21 resembles an appendix and is probably a later addition to the Gospel from an editor's hand

(Culpepper, pp. 5, 45ff). One reason for such views is that John 20.30f can be read quite naturally as providing the conclusion to the entire work that is John's Gospel; hence chapter 21 is made to stand apart as a separate unit, a supplement. But I prepared you for this possibility by my opening remarks on the suitability of this text as a working example.

Another textual question concerns verse 24 of this chapter (the detailed textual evidence can be seen in a commentary, such as Barrett, 1962, p. 489). Even if chapter 21 as a whole is integral to the original Gospel of John, it is felt that at least verse 24 must be an addition. This raises an interesting issue: does one trust scholarly instincts in excising a verse or more in the reconstruction of the original text, or does one need to see evidence such as an actual manuscript of the text where these words are lacking?

In the present instance, no manuscript is known to lack verse 24, but there are reasons to back the scholarly instincts. It looks as if it might be a formula of authorisation, consciously modelled on John 19.35.

> He who saw this has testified so that you also may believe. His testimony is true, and he knows/there is one who knows that he tells the truth.
>
> (19.35)

> This is the disciple who is testifying to these things and has written them/caused them to be written, and we know that his testimony is true.
>
> (21.24)

The alternative translation in 21.24 ('caused them to be written') and the highly significant use of the first person plural ('we know') give every impression of the apostolic Church verifying the original testimony with its seal of approval.

There are two further points where the text is disputed. Following 21.24 is one of several places where the floating episode (usually found within brackets at John 7.53–8.11), the story of the woman who had been caught in the act of adultery, is located in some manuscripts. This heightens the impression of chapter 21 as an appendix where additional items are collected. Finally, John 21.25: the whole verse is omitted in the important fourth-century manuscript Codex Sinaiticus. It could be argued that it is a crude repetition of John 20.30f:

Now Jesus did many other signs in the presence of his disciples, which are not written in this book. But these are written so that you may come to believe that Jesus is the Messiah, the Son of God, and that through believing you may have life in his name.

(20.30f)

But there are also many other things that Jesus did; if every one of them were written down, I suppose that the world itself could not contain the books that would be written.

(21.25)

STAGE 2: THE ACCURACY OF THE ENGLISH TRANSLATION (WHICHEVER IS USED)

To a certain extent the choice of a translation, in which to read the text, is a matter either of subjective preference or of the convenience of an edition which is to hand. But it is most important that a translation is used where any subtleties of original meaning are not obscured, either by the free and poetic nature of the language, or by the conscious use of a limited vocabulary. The chances are that a translation which has been 'improved' by a panel of literary experts, or has restricted itself to a small vocabulary in the interests of mass communication, will have incurred losses in historical accuracy as a rendering of the original. One must also be aware of the risk of doctrinal or ideological bias in translations of a particular persuasion.

Recent celebration of the achievements of William Tyndale, commemorating the five hundredth anniversary of his birth in 1494, has claimed that his 'New Testament of 1534 was taken over almost word for word by the editors of the Authorised Version of 1611. Where they departed from his original it was usually for the worse.' Ought we not to be on our guard, when we recognise that the historical basis of understanding in a translation which is still widely favoured for aesthetic reasons, is effectively 450 years old? Scholarship has moved a long way in that time.

Yet translation remains a process of communication, where the meaning is gathered with maximum accuracy at one end, and communicated with the maximum effectiveness at the other. Again, Tyndale may well have possessed 'an unerring ear for the authentic rhythm of English speech'. But to fix the forms of an English golden age is unlikely to ensure modernity in communication. Much has changed in English, and not just the spelling, in nearly five hundred years. One must beware of emotive assertions, based on aesthetic preferences, which talk of 'the shabby street of shame which is most modern biblical translation'.

To illustrate how different published translations may conjure up quite divergent impressions in the reader's mind, compare John 21.7–8 as translated by William Tyndale in 1526, and in the Authorised Version, with four modern translations:

Then sayde the disciple, whom Jesus loved, unto Peter, It is the Lorde. When Simon Peter herde that it was the Lorde, he gyrde his mantell to hym, for he was naked, and sprange into the see. The other disciples cam by shippe, for they were nott farre from londe, butt as itt were two hondred cubites, and they drewe the net with fisshes.

(Tyndale)

Therefore that disciple whom Jesus loved saith unto Peter, It is the Lord. Now when Simon Peter heard that it was the Lord, he girt his fisher's coat unto him, (for he was naked,) and did cast himself into the sea. And the other disciples came in a little ship; (for they were not far from land, but as it were two hundred cubits,) dragging the net with fishes.

(Authorised Version)

That disciple whom Jesus loved said to Peter, 'It is the Lord!' When Simon Peter heard that it was the Lord, he put on some clothes, for he was naked, and jumped into the sea. But the other disciples came in the boat, dragging the net full of fish, for they were not far from the land, only about a hundred yards off.

(New Revised Standard Version)

Then the disciple whom Jesus loved said to Peter, 'It is the Lord!' As soon as Simon Peter heard him say, 'It is the Lord,' he fastened his coat about him (for he had stripped) and plunged into the sea. The rest of them came on in the boat, towing the net full of fish. They were only about a hundred yards from land.

(Revised English Bible)

So the disciple whom Jesus loved said to Peter, 'It is the Lord.' When Simon Peter heard that it was the Lord, he tucked in his garment, for he was lightly clad, and jumped into the sea. The other disciples came in the boat, for they were not far from shore, only about a hundred yards, dragging the net with the fish.

(New American Bible)

The disciple whom Jesus loved said to Peter, 'It is the Lord.' At these words, 'It is the Lord,' Simon Peter tied his outer garment round him (for he had nothing on) and jumped into the water. The other disciples came on in the boat, towing the net with the fish, for they were only about a hundred yards from land.

(New Jerusalem Bible)

STAGE 3: THE LITERARY AND HISTORICAL BACKGROUND

At this stage attention is paid to fundamentally historical issues. These concern the glimpses that may be obtained by reading the text of this chapter: indications of the historical situation in which the story happens, indeed whether it can have happened like this; and the kind of literary critical questions (asked by a previous generation of scholars) about when, where, and by whom the story was written. There are several examples to give, as well as observations to be made.

The first observations are about authorship. The conventional criteria are matters of the style of writing and the vocabulary used – issues easier to determine in the original Greek than in translations. We might wish to decide on the basis of such criteria whether the author of John 21 is identical with the author of chapters 1–20. It is possible to make a list of words and expressions which only occur in chapter 21 within John's Gospel, but one would have to admit that the majority of these are not very significant, hardly the evidence required to prove a case beyond question. There might be evidence to point the other way, towards identity of authorship. One interesting feature occurs at John 21.18: the double use of 'amen amen' is characteristic of John's Gospel, but would of course be easy to imitate, if a new author wished to add material in the style of the old.

A recent observation about the continuing discussion on the dating of John 21, in relation to the rest of the Gospel, is by Robert Morgan:

The dating of John is also disputed and now complicated by the widespread recognition of a lengthy process of composition, but there is no good reason to dispute a final date, with ch. 21 included, in the 90s.

(1994, p. 9)

It is all too easy to move across from firmer evidence about date and authorship to rather subjective speculation about the kind of author with whom one might be dealing. Would the same author add material to his Gospel in so clumsy a way, without the obvious remedy of moving John 20.31f to the new ending of his extended work? However, an equally clumsy survival can be found in the last words of John 14.31, now in the middle of a discourse. Not quite so speculative, but still subjective, is the attempt to characterise the author of John 21 on the basis of the ideas contained in his chapter. Is he a careful and sensitive harmoniser of the Jesus-traditions of the Johannine Church, while being a less profound theologian than the author of the fourth Gospel? Perhaps he is the same author as wrote one or more of the Johannine letters, texts which according to several commentators (e.g. J.L. Houlden) might again indicate a less elevated but more pragmatic theology?

Another kind of speculative reconstruction, which has become much more common in recent years, is the characterisation of the audience for whom the literary text appeared to be intended. A more modern kind of literary criticism is concerned with the readers and their ideal or actual responses to a text. This fresh interest has reanimated the older speculation. Some possible indications of the audience will emerge as we examine the function of the story (see below, in stage 5), or as we now turn to comment on clues to the geographical and historical setting of John 21.

Several aspects of this story of a fishing expedition foster a sense of realism in this historical and geographical setting. The story suits the Palestinian context. Night is the time for fishing, as fishing boats equipped with lights on the Sea of Galilee, and widely in the Mediterranean, demonstrate even today. (On the other hand, one should not forget the symbolic importance of night as the time of Satan in John's Gospel – see John 13.27,30. Small wonder that the disciples caught nothing!) Fishing is a task sensibly performed while near-naked (21.7). To greet someone, however, is a religious act which could not be performed unclothed. You would not normally greet people when you met at the baths and everyone was naked (see Jerusalem Talmud *Berakoth* 2,4c, 38). Finally what Jesus does at 21.13 is the act of the host, invoking the blessing at a Jewish meal. Such features may well favour historicity, but could be explained as the fruits of literary realism.

A story may have several contexts. There may be signs of authenticity to do with the original situation of an event. But there is also the context (one or several perhaps) when the story is recounted in relation to new circumstances. There may be aspects of the new situation that are at odds with the original circumstances. So the social setting of John 21 may reflect the original call by Jesus of disciples who were once fishermen (see Mark 1.16–20; Luke 5.1–11). But their resumption of fishing at this point certainly seems implausible historically, as a sequel to their commissioning for other tasks at John 20.21ff. Notice, however, that in the figurative and symbolic sense (see stage 6, below) 'going fishing' is entirely consistent with that mission charge in John 20 and Mark 1.17.

It may well be possible to identify a social situation for the recounting of this story, to give it a place in history, as well as a rationale in timeless symbolism. The clue is provided by John 21.23:

> So the rumour spread in the community that this disciple would not die. Yet Jesus did not say to him that he would not die, but,'If it is my will that he remain until I come, what is that to you?'

Had 'the disciple whom Jesus loved' died unexpectedly, and so the account in the second half of John 21 was to square the matter? As Raymond Brown writes:

> The obvious import of the saying [John 21.22] is that Jesus will return during that [Beloved] Disciple's lifetime, and this is how Christians interpreted it (21.23). But since the Beloved Disciple was dying or dead by the time John 21 was written, the Johannine author of chapter 21 employs casuistry to show that Jesus' promise was not absolute.
>
> (1994, p. 55)

The tradition of John 21.23 may be very early in the community's consciousness, while verses 24f belong to the latest stage of the Gospel.

Sociologists say that, within a religious community where there is a living tradition of prophecy, an apparently unfulfilled prophecy is reinterpreted by the community, so as to reflect their actual situation more closely. The perspective of 'misleading' prophecy is adjusted, to cope with the actual disappointment. The sociological label 'cognitive dissonance' has been used to describe this (see Robert Carroll's studies of the prophet Jeremiah *When Prophecy Failed*). The splendid novel by Alison Lurie entitled *Imaginary Friends* illustrates both the social situation, which broadly resembles that of the disappointed Johannine community, and also the sociological method in action.

There is one more detail in the text which could provide a clue to a historical setting. John 21.18 may well be a proverbial saying (see below, stage 4). But, taken together with the explanatory comment of verse 19, it could well provide evidence of this Christian community's knowledge that Peter was martyred by crucifixion. If so, John 21 should be compared with another Johannine text, Revelation 11.7f, where the description of the two witnesses' fate can very reasonably be interpreted as the deaths of Peter and Paul at Rome in the days of the Emperor Nero (sometime between 64 and 68 CE). Such a tradition may be maintained in their joint feast day, 29 June. In contrast, John 21 suggests a different kind of association, this time between the respective fates of Peter and the Beloved Disciple.

STAGE 4: SOURCE OF THE STORY OF JESUS' APPEARANCE BY THE LAKE

The literary exercise of source criticism, applied to an apparently self-contained unit of the size of John 21, might well involve separating out strands of the narrative (for this see stage 5, below). But the principal task is to trace back the present form of the story to earlier stages in the flow of the tradition. It resembles walking upstream beside a river, in the hope of finding the source. In literary terms one is dependent on identifying rough edges, or forms of narrative analogous to others already well known, to assist in a (partly conjectural) reconstruction of an earlier text.

It is often said that John 21.4–14 derives from a 'signs source' (a prototype Johannine collection of material on the miracles of Jesus, found between chapters 2 and 11). John 21.15–23 would then come from a different source. As a dialogue between Jesus and Peter, it may be the reworking of a traditional conversation, or else be modelled on the pattern of the dialogues and discourses at the Last Supper in chapters 13–17 of John's Gospel. This identification of twin sources for our text might raise an interesting suggestion: the author of the literary epilogue in John 21 by combining these elements has imitated deliberately the combined structure of signs and discourses in the whole Gospel.

There are three further observations about the source of John 21, which are probably more helpful as illustrations of method than as confirmation of any conclusion. The first concerns the relation between our text and the Gospel of Luke. This could be part of a larger, and highly disputed, question about the relation of John to this one of the synoptic Gospels. But the particular issue is whether Luke provides either the source or an earlier parallel tradition for the story in John 21. One needs to look at the relationship to Luke 5.1–11 (which records a similarly miraculous catch of fish, but is not chronicled as happening after the resurrection), and also to Luke 24.13–35 (which is a post-resurrection appearance of Jesus, involving a meal with a strongly eucharistic aspect, but is not concerned with fishing).

A second observation draws attention to a parallel with the apocryphal Gospel of Peter. Such Gospel texts are now being examined as possible sources about Jesus with a measure of independence from the New Testament; but they used to be regarded as secondary derivatives from and supplements to the canonical Gospels. To say the least, the relationship is problematic. It concerns us now because there is a rough parallel to John 21.2 at the end of the Gospel of Peter just before the fragmentary text breaks off:

> But I, Simon Peter, and my brother Andrew took our nets and went to the sea. And there was with us Levi, the son of Alphaeus, whom the Lord . . .
>
> (14(60))

If one is simply classifying the accounts of post-resurrection appearances of Jesus in the canonical and apocryphal traditions, one should notice the usual distinction between those set in Jerusalem and those set in Galilee. John 21 and Peter 60 clearly belong to the Galilee tradition, whereas John 20 and the previous section of Peter belong in Jerusalem. Are both seeking to harmonise two originally separate traditions?

A third observation is the most radical of all. It was a suggestion made by Rudolf Bultmann in his commentary that the story has its original basis in the proverb still preserved in the text at 21.18:

> Very truly, I tell you, when you were younger, you used to

fasten your own belt and to go wherever you wished. But when you grow old, you will stretch out your hands, and someone else will fasten a belt around you and take you where you do not wish to go.

In this final form of the developed story, the references to Peter are made specific, to his impulsive activity (see 21.7), and to the ending of his life. The central importance of the proverb, as applied to the story it has generated, is shown by the solemn 'double amen' which introduces the verse. In contrast, the original proverb would have had a much more general reference, such as: In youth man goes free, where he wishes; in old age he must allow himself to be led, even where he does not wish.

For a Wisdom saying of similar character one could compare Psalm 37.25:

I have been young, and now am old, yet have I not seen the righteous forsaken or their children begging bread.

Interestingly there is a verbal echo between Psalm 37.25 and John 21.18: in the Greek both texts use the word 'younger' to mean 'young' (such a use of the comparative adjective is a natural Greek expression).

STAGE 5: FORM AND FUNCTION OF THE STORY

It is logical to look first at one aspect of the story's form. This is the possible roughness and inconsistency of the present ingredients, which might suggest that two originally separate narratives have been combined here, but a little clumsily. It might be necessary to think of different functions for the separate strands, as well as the ultimate purpose of the combined stories.

A critical reader could be worried by inconsistencies in the flow of the narrative as it stands. Like the account in Luke 5.1–11, this narrative has the form of a miracle story. It is a miracle because the disciples themselves had tried hard, but had caught no fish. Following Jesus' instructions the catch is miraculous in its abundance. But it scarcely seems necessary because, when the disciples come to land, there is fish already cooking. Yet the disciples are still told to bring fish from their catch for the breakfast.

A further factor in the analysis is the variety of vocabulary. Three different words are used for 'fish', as well as two words for 'love', two for 'feed', and two or three for 'sheep'.

agapao, phileo	'love'
prosphagion, ichthus, opsarion	'fish'
boske, poimaine	'feed'
arnia, probatia	'sheep'

(with the variation, *probata*, as in John 10)

Incidentally this emphasises the reason why a translation ideally requires a wide vocabulary, in order not to conceal such variations from the non-Greek reader. It is by no means clear how these variations in language would correspond to different sources underlying a combined narrative. There could well be other explanations, such as variety for the sake of a good literary style. One needs to decide whether John used near-synonyms for literary reasons, or deliberately to signal different senses.

To take the first pair of variants for 'love': some say these words are straightforward synonyms in the fourth Gospel; others claim that one word is selected, rather than the other, for theological not literary reasons. For example, John 21.15–17 has been interpreted in this way. After his denial of Jesus, Peter is being challenged at three successive levels (in descending order): is Peter's love stronger than others'; is it the selfless love of Christ himself; or can it even be challenged at the level of friendship which is all that Peter is prepared to claim? In turn, Jesus' response is correspondingly constructive, commissioning Peter in important matters, significantly including the affectionate diminutive word (*probatia*) for the 'sheep' at 21.16 and 17.

If we consider the whole text of chapter 21 as a unit, either as an original entity, or in a final form as a construct from separate stories, we should ask, What is the purpose of this narrative as a unit? What would its function be? There are several suggestions to be explored.

Here we are dealing with longer-term motives, and even with the politics of relationship between Church communities. Firstly, this chapter may signal something about the relationship between Peter and the Beloved Disciple (John?) as Church leaders. In contrast to the impression of competition that is conveyed by John 20.3–8 (the story of the race to the tomb which emphasises the relative merits of speed and insight), the message in John 21 is of essential partnership.

It is important to realise that John 21.24, referring to 'these things', coordinates Jesus' prophecies in this chapter about Peter and the Beloved Disciple. Peter will be pastor, leader and martyr in the Church. John 21.22 may indicate a vestigial rebuke, but overall this chapter takes a high view of Peter; he will be chief pastor, just as he took the lead in going fishing (21.3). The beloved disciple is different – he will not be a martyr, but he will be a witness, and indeed is responsible for the whole content of 'witness' – that is, testimony or evidence in preaching, supplied in this Gospel. This could well be a partnership of complementary types of Church leader.

Others have suggested not so much an equal partnership, more a stress on the superiority of the Beloved Disciple. Should one see Peter's impetuosity at John 21.7 as comparable to his confession at Caesarea Philippi (Mark 8.29)? One knows with the hindsight of the New Testament reader that what followed the impetuous confession was Jesus' rebuke (Mark 8.33) and Peter's threefold denial (Mark 14.66–72; although other traditions, such as Matthew 16.17–19 and Luke 22.31f are already mitigating this aspect of Peter's 'failure'). By comparison, the Beloved Disciple is the one who 'saw and believed' (John 20.8). At the end of the text, it is this disciple whose testimony is vouched for by the community (John 21.24).

But overall the idea of unfavourable comparison is not strong in John 21. And we must notice that the comparative expression in 21.15 ('more than these') is not singular (more than the Beloved Disciple) but plural. This plural may relate to the other disciples in general (more than they do?); but it could be 'more than these things' – that is, the attractions of fishing!

Another suggestion mentioned already (see stage 3) should not be forgotten. This chapter belongs in the situation of crisis caused by the deaths of the first eye-witness generation, and of the Beloved Disciple in particular. The principal motive for the addition of this chapter would appear to be indicated by 21.23–4. The intention was, by an explanation of Jesus' words in the mouth of the Lord himself, to provide a substitute for the older view which held that the Beloved Disciple would survive until Parousia. If an imminent expectation, comparable to that of Mark 9.1, was disappointed, then the Johannine community came to terms with the disappointment by this rationalisation of the disciple's role.

There is an important emphasis here on the social function of this text. To appreciate this fully would require a much more complete reconstruction of the social setting than is possible within the evidence of this chapter alone. It is tempting to supply a larger context from the Gospel, the Johannine letters and even the Book of Revelation. If one thinks of a 'community of the Beloved Disciple', a group of Johannine Christians with a history reflected across these texts, then the focus may be a quite small group, marginalised by society or consciously separating itself in a 'monastic' manner. They emphasise that their inspiration comes from the original vision of how Christianity should be 'at the beginning'.

This is to read into our text evidence that is mostly external to it. But there are a few indicators within chapter 21 which might corroborate some aspects of the picture. A group conscious of its origins and basic inspiration might well characterise that in terms of the call, and repeated call, of Galilean disciples. We see within the story of the fishing expedition, a community at a loss, desolated by the absence of Jesus. The community of the Beloved Disciple replicates this situation by its desolation at the loss of their own leader. The function of the story is deliberately to restore the original confidence, and to rebuild a group devastated by unexpected events. This would centre the community afresh on Jesus ('It is the Lord' – John 21.7), rather than upon the founding fathers or upon alternative teachers and salvation systems.

A further suggestion might follow from this, in the longer term. The ultimate function of John 21, in relation to the whole Gospel and the other Johannine writings, would be to provide dominical and ecclesiastical guarantees for the Johannine tradition. The historical setting of this would be one of polemic between the Churches as to which Gospel tradition should hold the priority. Such a conflict might well have existed between the tradition of John and that of Mark (which claimed the authority of Peter). Each tradition would have its geographical regions of support, sustained by local Churches.

But it is unlikely, although sometimes suggested, that we should see embodied in such a conflict the rivalries of the later Quartodeciman controversy about the date when Easter should be celebrated in the Churches. Should the Christians follow the Jewish practice about Passover and so always celebrate Easter on Nisan 14, whatever day of the week this was? Or should it be the Sunday following, since Sunday was regarded as the weekly 'day of resurrection'? Peter would then stand for the latter practice in Rome and the West, while John and Asia Minor were regarded as the authority for the Quartodeciman practice in the East. In 155 CE Polycarp, bishop of Smyrna in Asia Minor, tried to persuade Rome to follow the Eastern practice. Pope Anicetus refused, but tolerated the alternative practice. Thirty or forty years later Pope Victor took a more rigid line and excommunicated Polycrates, bishop of Ephesus, for his refusal to conform. If John 21 were being used as a weapon in this controversy, one feels that such specific issues would have been indicated more clearly in the text. This remains true, even though modern scholarship is concerned about divergencies over the timing of the Last Supper between John and the synoptic Gospels. Here it is a difference of timing between Nisan 14 and Nisan 15 – another chronological controversy about Easter, but a different one.

Finally, as an indication of an alternative viewpoint: it might seem perverse to read John 21 with a focus on rivalry between Peter and the Beloved Disciple. With the words 'Follow me', Jesus led Peter off to continue the conversation. But Peter's attention strayed from Christ to the uninvited Beloved Disciple. Both parts of Christ's reply serve to turn Peter back to his Lord, whose will is what matters and whose person must be Peter's prime concern (21.22). Derek Kidner, whose exposition this is, concludes: 'It is interesting that his [Peter's] fellow Christians failed to get the point, speculating about John (*sic*) in spite of Christ's "What is that to you?"' (Scripture Union Daily Notes 1994).

STAGE 6: DOUBLE MEANINGS: ALLEGORY AND SYMBOLISM

It has already been mentioned (in stage 3) that 'going fishing' (21.3) could carry a figurative sense, instead of or as well as the literal one. This would make the story consistent with the mission charge of John 20.21,

> Peace be with you. As the Father has sent me, so I send you.

rather than an act of rebellion. The idea of fishing as an image for apostolic mission could be derived from a text like Mark 1.17:

> And Jesus said to them, 'Follow me and I will make you fish for people.'

The very familiarity of the Christian symbol of the fish, and mission choruses about 'Fishers of men', should not allow us to forget that this idea originated with texts such as these. Previously, in Old Testament terms, 'catching men' has the bad sense we associate with confidence trickery. So are new symbols created by fresh thinking.

As part of the same imagery of fishing as mission, the Greek word translated as 'haul' at John 21.6 and 11 is the same word that is rendered as 'draw' at John 6.44 and 12.32, and used of drawing men to Christ. So this is a metaphorical use found elsewhere in John's Gospel. When it comes to the contents of the net which Peter hauled ashore, 153 large fish, we must ask if the symbolism is maintained consistently. In the Syrian Orthodox exegesis, these 'large' fish are identified with the great patriarchs of the Church. They represent the fulness of the Christian Church, which shows that the harvest of the world-sea is nearly complete. On the number itself, many biblical commentators would agree with C.K. Barrett:

> The number is significant or it would not have been recorded; it is improbable that it represents the fortuitous but precise recollection of an eye-witness.

> (1962, p. 484; 1978, p. 581)

So in what does its significance consist?

Mathematically 153 is an interesting number, for three reasons. Firstly, it is a curious fact that 'when the cubes of the digits of any 3-digit number that is a multiple of 3 are added, and then this process is repeated, the final result is 153, where the process ends, because $153 = 1^3 + 5^3 + 3^3$' (Wells, *Penguin Dictionary of Curious and Interesting Numbers*, p. 140). Secondly, 153 is the sum of the factorial numbers 1! to 5! (i.e. = 1!+2!+3!+4!+5!). Factorial 5 (denoted by 5!) is the product of $5 \times 4 \times 3 \times 2 \times 1 = 120$. And thirdly, it is the triangular number of 17 (the sum of the numbers 1–17).

That the number 153 appealed to the author of John 21 seems plain. A modern writer, W.E. Bowman, used this same number to excess in his humorous novel *The Ascent of Rum Doodle*. But which mathematical reason explains the appeal to symbolism is debatable. The Pythagoreans had associated 5 with marriage, as the sum of 2 (female) and 3 (male), but this is scarcely relevant to John 21. Talk of a 3-digit number which equals the sum of the cubes of its own digits might suggest a Trinitarian explanation, but for the fact that the Christian doctrine of the Trinity is a later formulation.

This leaves the third fact about the number 17. Seventeen is the sum of 10 and 7. Does 10 stand for the Ten Commandments of the

Old Testament and 7 for the gifts of the Spirit (Isaiah 11.2f LXX; Romans 12.6–8; Ephesians 4.7–12), as they do in the folksong? Rather than as explicit symbols for the two testaments, it might be better to see both 7 and 10 as indicating completeness and perfection. The double combination then intensifies the symbol, which could represent most fully the final total of Church membership. This would be analogous to the way that 144,000 is used inclusively rather than exclusively of the number of those sealed and saved in Revelation 7.

STAGE 7: APPLICATIONS IN MODERN EXPOSITIONS

The final stage in this process of practical exploration in our sample text is to identify those ideas and images which might appropriately be carried forward into contemporary interpretations, sermons and artistic developments. In this way symbols take on a new lease of life, and historical situations assume new relevance.

It is not too surprising, given what can be surmised about the circumstances of John 21, that the majority of applications concern Church life and practice. Emphasis on the strategy for mission would seem to match well with the underlying symbolism of the text. But there are also concerns for the structures of Church leadership, perhaps recognising the complementarity of different styles of leadership (Peter and the Beloved Disciple). In the context of John's Gospel the role model for the Church leader is that of shepherd (John 21.15–17, following the example of the Good Shepherd – 10.1–16, 26). This is a pervasive image of Christian ministry and pastoral care (see Acts 20.28f; 1 Peter 5.2–4). It is also an Old Testament image, as in Ezekiel, where good shepherds are praised and the wicked shepherds castigated.

Probably the most dramatic structural pattern to be found in this text is the one which helps to emphasise this idea of leadership as shepherding. A favourite sermon theme, drawing this out, concentrates on Peter's threefold affirmation, and accompanying charge to tend the flock, and its contrast with Peter's triple denial of Jesus (John 18.17, 25–7).

Within the Christian tradition of sacramental meals, such as the Eucharist as a memorial of the Last Supper, the episodes concerning meals with the risen Christ occupy a special place. The breakfast on the shore of John 21 shares with the meal at Emmaus (Luke 24.30) this significance as teaching 'patterns'. In the tradition of the fourth

Gospel, the use (at least in symbolic terms) of fish as well as bread at the Eucharist is attested by John 6.9, where the miraculous feeding with the ensuing discourse incorporates later sacramental ideas.

There could be a further reference to a Christian sacrament in John 21.7, where Peter plunges into the water. The combination of ideas about water and nakedness can be associated with primitive Church traditions about undressing and dressing in a new garment for baptismal initiation (e.g. Galatians 3.27). Similar ideas about baptism can be found in John 13.6–10 in the setting of the Last Supper. Just as the young man in Mark 14.51f has been thought by some (e.g. Morton Smith) to represent an initiate into a mystical group associated with Jesus, so Peter, in John 21, would be initiated by the Beloved Disciple who enables Peter to 'put on the vision of Christ'.

Another theme of the narrative of John 21, more often overlooked, is the failure of the disciples to recognise Jesus (2.4). Again the close comparison is with Luke 24.31 in the meal at Emmaus; it seems to be a feature of the resurrection stories in particular that the Eucharist is the means of Christ's self-disclosure. The tradition of apparently dim-witted disciples has been recognised as an uncomfortable feature of Mark's Gospel. It conforms to modern awareness of a widespread lack of spiritual enlightenment; there is correspondingly greater rejoicing at the appearance of someone with the insight to recognise the deeper truth (see 21.7). The task of Christian discipleship is seen as a matter of 'following' here (21.19, 22), just as it is in John 12.25f and also consistently in the teaching of Mark's Gospel (see Mark 8.34f).

Perhaps the last word should be with Stephen S. Smalley who sees John 21 as 'setting out an agenda for the Church in the future, on the basis of the exaltation of Jesus' (1994, p. 66).

Postscript: Ariadne's thread – an essay in deconstruction

If you visit the ancient site of Knossos just south of Heraklion in Crete, you will find the results of Minoan archaeology laid out before you in the substantially reconstructed palace of the priest-king Minos. Knossos owes much to the interpretative flair and enthusiasm of the British archaeologist Arthur Evans who lived and worked there in the early years of this century. Evans identified the rooms, restored their decorations and made this palace come alive. He even overcame what might have seemed a fatal flaw to his identification. Where were the grand state apartments one might expect to find in such a palace complex? They must have been on the upper floor which collapsed when the palace was destroyed by earthquake and fire in the fourteenth century BCE.

Evans's style of working has been criticised by later archaeologists, some of whom have contested his identifications. Hans Wunderlich (*The Secret of Crete*, 1975) argued that it was not a royal palace, but a large-scale cemetery (a necropolis, or city of the dead). On the contrary, it was neither palace nor necropolis, but rather what mythology had always said it was – a labyrinth. According to Rodney Castleden (*The Knossos Labyrinth: A New View of the 'Palace of Minos' at Knossos*, 1990) it was a large temple and religious centre, a maze of cultic rooms surrounding the courtyard of the man-bull, the Minotaur.

In the ancient Greek mythology of the Cretan labyrinth, Ariadne (the daughter of King Minos) plays a significant role. She fell in love with Theseus the hero of Athens when he came to Crete to face the Minotaur. The Minotaur had been born of the union of the god Poseidon's white bull with Pasiphae, Minos's wife. Ariadne, as the daughter of Pasiphae and Minos, was thus half-sister to the monster. But with Ariadne's assistance Theseus was able to escape after he had killed the bull; she provided him with the vital clue of a magic thread to enable him to find his way safely out of the labyrinth. They fled together, but for some reason (variously conjectured) he abandoned her on the island of Naxos while she lay sleeping. (Sleeping Ariadne is a perennial motif for surrealist painting, initiated by De Chirico.)

Like other ancient myths the story of Theseus and Ariadne has been explained and 'decoded' in various ways. It is thought that Ariadne may have been a local goddess on Naxos, a regional variant of Aphrodite with whom she was later syncretised. Robert Graves refers to the Troy Town mazes of neolithic times, and to ritual dances of a labyrinthine type, some involving a thread which is held by the dancers (*The Greek Myths*, section 98). The myth is also held to have a deeper meaning, to justify its use in ancient society, whether in cosmological or psychological terms. It may be a Greek version of the pattern of royal succession which seems to entail the ritual death of the king. Here Theseus is revolutionary and breaks the pattern because he escapes from death. But it may also be a variation on the frequent mythic theme of the descent into the underworld, showing what may and may not be retrieved from that situation.

Such stories can have a psychological interpretation. As Heinrich Zimmer in *The King and the Corpse* argued:

> The quality that finally saves the kingly personage – the Ariadne thread that guides him through the labyrinth of the interior night – is the sincerity of his willingness to endure the enterprise, his courage in the toils of the demon powers let loose upon him. This sustains him against the enigmatic questions.
>
> (1971, pp. 225f)

In the terms of Jungian psychoanalysis, the maze is the unconscious; the Minotaur stands for various forces, particularly the dark shadow, so that to kill the Minotaur represents a decisive release; and Ariadne is the 'anima' – that is, the conscious sexual aspect of the psyche. The thread can be a parable of personal inner certainty, not necessarily entailing intellectual clarity: after all Theseus had to grope in the dark rather than march through a lighted space (see Barnaby and D'Acieno, 1990).

When a modern reader encounters a myth, or any other genre of text, the situation closely resembles that of the visitor to Knossos encountering the remains of this important archaeological site. For the text, just as for the site, a wide variety of interpretations is theoretically possible, to match the evidence before one. The basic structure can be 'read' (detected, deciphered and analysed) in several ways. Much will depend upon the reader's initial expectations and presuppositions. Most people will see the traces of what they were expecting to see. So it was when modern monks interpreted the remains at Qumran as those of an ancient monastery, and academics took them to be those of a school! Sometimes a 'reader' makes great use of the creative imagination in order to communicate powerfully to others, and to help them to see more clearly just what it was desired for them to see. So it was with Sir Arthur Evans at Knossos.

It is possible to assemble a catalogue of the available meanings for a text that have been suggested to date. This would resemble the list of interpretations (palace, necropolis, labyrinth) proposed for Knossos. Each 'reading' can be annotated according to the situation of the person who makes the interpretation. There may well be a close correlation between the reading and the context of the interpreter. It may be much less likely that one can identify a living relationship or essential continuity between the whole range of interpretations to be found in the catalogue. There could be a consistent pattern between readings from within the same cultural tradition. But a new attitude necessarily creates a new perspective which breaks the pattern. It may be that abandoned readings somehow still affect the new reading, like hidden strata under our feet.

Furthermore we cannot be sure that our catalogue of available readings will bear much, if any, relationship to the attitudes and intentions of the originator of the literary text or of the historical building. It is one thing to presume that there was an author/architect who had a specific purpose or design; it is a very different matter to assume either that the original purpose corresponds to the interpretations of a later generation, or even that it is still possible to discover the original purpose.

The inevitable consequence is a multiplicity of readings with no guarantee of consistency or compatibility between them. Even an authoritative text, such as from the Bible, can speak in totally different ways to different epochs. Are we to locate any concept of divine inspiration at the original point of 'dictation' or authorship; or does it belong at each and every occurrence of interpretation and communication of meaning to a new audience?

The ultimate stages of academic perception, in terms of cultural relativity and literary deconstruction, seem to sap what confidence remains for a definitive interpretation and a plain meaning of the text. 'Authorial and textual plurality create a labyrinth from which there appears to be no exit' (Taylor, 1982, p. 61). The role of the author in relation to his or her writings has been redefined. Authors have become self-denying, like the prompter in the theatre whose real aim in life is to be unnecessary, to do himself or herself out of a job. The author essentially becomes a reader of those works which he or she thought to have originated. Does this then make the readers into authors?

Certainly the act of reading and interpretation is regarded as intrinsic to any moment of a text's coming into being. And every text is a labyrinth of interpenetrating interpretations. The theological model of incarnation can be seen as closely related to the existence of Scripture. Just as the disembodied idea of *logos* (word) is re-expressed in the particular divine self-realisation in the span of a human life, which in turn communicates itself through other human lives, so the embodied word is inscribed in a powerful text whose power consists both in its being written and in its rewriting which must itself be rewritten.

It seems to me to be more than a happy coincidence that a writer on deconstruction from a theological (or should it be atheological?) perspective, such as the American Mark C. Taylor (1982, 1984), can use the language of the Theseus legend – the labyrinth and Ariadne's thread – and use it so expressively. He reminds his readers of the influence of death of God theology, and certainly regards deconstruction as the hermeneutic of the death of God. One can even forgive the characteristic verbal punning in the reference to 'mazing grace' – instead of salvation we have the idea of a labyrinth with no Ariadne.

But Taylor himself has provided a theological Ariadne's thread – complicated as it is by the paradoxical ideas associated with *logos* and word, incarnation and resurrection, which the Christian tradition has employed from the early years. Is the route of the thought so contorted that the thread breaks? The modern experience may well resemble being lost in a maze, helpless to extricate oneself. But Taylor's overwhelming and bewildering sense of plurality is rendered intelligible, and essentially communicable to others, by exactly those linkages of thought, those pairings of contrasted or complementary ideas, that are self-explanatory associations. At least this may work in the particular context, the intellectual microcosm. The question is, does it work in the macrocosm of the total theological and cultural experience of living? Either there is an Ariadne's thread or there isn't.

The present reader, from his own admittedly subjective and localised viewpoint, prefers to believe that there is a connecting and redeeming thread – however tangled and obscured it may be sometimes. Apparent obscurity may be the main problem; but, as for Theseus, there seems to exist a kind of guarantee that the thread is actually supple, stong and reliable. It is always necessary to ask oneself what grounds one has for confidence in an authoritative reading, even for reading life as a text. If we recognise the existence of a multiplicity of threads, this surely implies that not all of them can be equally valid for us. But rather than insist that we have the monopoly of the only real thread – so that we have certainty while everyone else has bewilderment – instead we should hold to what we discover to be the more reliable thread, while recognising that all around there is a tangle of other, possibly misleading, threads. There are moments of disclosure and perception. As Wallace Stevens declared, new possibilities of order and vision are always awaiting us:

> We live in a constellation
> Of patches and of pitches,
> Not in a single world,
> In things said well in music,
> On the piano, and in speech,
> As in a page of poetry –
> Thinkers without final thoughts
> In an incipient cosmos,
> The way, when we climb a mountain,
> Vermont throws itself together.

'July Mountain'

NOTE

This chapter originally appeared in *Theology* in January 1991 and is reproduced here with permission.

Select bibliography

Barnaby, K. and D'Acieno, P. (eds) (1990) *Jung and the Humanities*, Routledge, London.

Barnes, Julian (1989) *A History of the World in 10½ Chapters*, Jonathan Cape, London.

Barrett, C.K. (1962, 2nd edition 1978) *The Gospel According to St. John*, SPCK, London.

Berlin, Adele (1983) *Poetics and the Interpretation of Biblical Narrative*, Almond Press, Sheffield.

Best, Ernest (1988) *Paul and His Converts*, T. & T. Clark, Edinburgh.

Bloom, Harold (1989) *Ruin the Sacred Truths*, Harvard UP, Cambridge Mass./London.

—— (1991) *The Book of J*, Faber & Faber, London.

Bradbury, Malcolm (ed.) (1987) *The Penguin Book of Modern British Short Stories*, Penguin, Harmondsworth.

Brown, G. and Yule, G. (1981) *Discourse Analysis*, Cambridge University Press, Cambridge.

Brown, Raymond (1994) *An Introduction to New Testament Christology*, Chapman/Mowbray.

Brueggeman, Walter (1986) 'The Costly Loss of Lament', *Journal for the Study of the Old Testament*, 36.

Bufalino, Gesualdo (1994) *The Keeper of the Ruins*, Harvill (Harper Collins), London.

Bultmann, Rudolf (1971) *The Gospel of John, A Commentary*, tr. G.R. Beasley Murray, Blackwell, Oxford.

Carroll, Robert (1979) *When Prophecy Failed*, SCM Press, London.

Castelli, Elizabeth A. (1991) *Imitating Paul: A Discourse of Power*, Westminster Press.

Castleden, Rodney (1990) *The Knossos Labyrinth: A New View of the 'Palace of Minos' at Knossos*, Routledge, London.

Chatman, Seymour (1978) *Story and Discourse*, Cornell University Press.

Corbett, Edward P.J. (1990) *Classical Rhetoric for the Modern Student*, Oxford University Press, New York.

Crispin, Edmund (1948) *Buried for Pleasure*, Gollancz, London.

Crossan, J.D. (1980) *Cliffs of Fall*, Seabury Press, New York.

—— (1986) *Saying Parallels – A Workbook for the Jesus Tradition*, Fortress Press, Philadelphia.

Culpepper, R. Alan (1983) *Anatomy of the Fourth Gospel*, Fortress Press, Philadelphia.

Dennett, Daniel C. (1992) *Consciousness Explained*, Allen Lane, London.

Dewey, Joanna (1980) *Markan Public Debate*, Scholars Press.

Dillistone, F.W. (1977) *C.H. Dodd – Interpreter of the New Testament*, Hodder & Stoughton, London.

Douglas, Lloyd C. (1942) *The Robe*, Houghton Mifflin.

Drummond, Sir William (1866) *The Oedipus Judaicus*, Reeves & Turner, London.

Ellul, Jacques (1975) *The New Demons*, Mowbray, London.

Fenton, John (1992) 'John of the Cross and the Gospel According to Mark', The Seventh Eric Symes Abbott Memorial Lecture, Westminster Abbey, 7 May, Englang Publishing, Cirencester, p. 8.

Fowler, Robert M. (1991) *Let the Reader Understand: Reader-Response Criticism and the Gospel of Mark*, Fortress Press, Minneapolis.

Gardner-Smith, P. (1938) *St John and the Synoptic Gospels*, Cambridge University Press, Cambridge.

Garrow, Alan (1997) *Revelation*, Routledge, London.

Heller, Joseph (1984) *God Knows*, Jonathan Cape, London.

Heym, Stefan (1973) *The King David Report*, Penguin Books, London.

Hollenweger, Walter J. (1982) *Conflict in Corinth*, Paulist Press, New York/Ramsey.

Hooker, Morna (1990) *From Adam to Christ*, Cambridge University Press, Cambridge.

Hopkins, Julie (1995) *Towards a Feminist Christology*, SPCK, London.

Iser, Wolfgang (1980) 'The Reading Process: A Phenomenological Approach', in Jane P. Tompkins (ed.) *Reader-Response Criticism. From Formalism to Post-Structuralism*, Johns Hopkins University Press, Baltimore.

Jacobson, Dan (1973) *The Rape of Tamar*, Penguin Books, London.

—— (1992) *The God-Fearer*, Bloomsbury Publishing Ltd, London.

Jung, C.G. (1952) *Answer to Job*, republished in 1994 by Routledge, London.

Kingsbury, Jack Dean (1986) *Matthew as Story*, Fortress Press, Philadelphia.

Kermode, Frank (1979) *Genesis of Secrecy*, Harvard UP, Cambridge Mass./London.

—— (1994) *New York Review of Books*, 24 March.

Kitzberger, Ingrid Rosa (1994) 'Love and Footwashing: John 13.1–20 and Luke 7.36–50 Read Intertextually', *Biblical Interpretation*, 2.2.

Knox, John (1959) *Philemon among the Letters of Paul*, Collins, London.

Lambrecht, Jan (1989) 'Rhetorical Criticism and the New Testament', *Bijdragen, Tijdschrift voor Filosofie en Theologie*, 50, pp. 239–53.

Lane Fox, Robin (1991) *The Unauthorized Version*, Viking, London.

Lightfoot, R.H. (1938) *Locality and Doctrine in the Gospels*, Hodder & Stoughton, London.

Lurie, Alison (1995) *Imaginary Friends*, Minerva, London.

Mack, Burton L. (1987) *A Myth of Innocence: Mark and Christian Origins*, Fortress Press, Philadelphia.

Magonet, Jonathan (1992) *Bible Lives*, SCM Press, London.

Malbon, Elizabeth Struthers (1991) *Narrative Space and Mythic Meaning in Mark*, JSOT Press, Sheffield.

—— (1992) 'Narrative Criticism: How Does the Story Mean?', in J.C. Anderson and S.D. Moore (eds) *Mark and Method: New Approaches in Biblical Studies*, Fortress Press, Minneapolis, pp. 23–49.

Meeks, Wayne (1983) *The First Urban Christians*, Yale University Press, London and New Haven, CT.

Mitchison, Naomi (1974/1924) *The Triumph of Faith*, in *When the Bough Breaks*, Bodley Head, London.

Moore, S.D. (1989) *Literary Criticism and the Gospels: The Theoretical Challenge*, Yale University Press, London and New Haven, CT.

Morgan, Robert (1994) 'Which was the Fourth Gospel?', *Journal for the Study of the New Testament*, 54, pp. 3–28.

Muilenburg, James (1969) 'Form Criticism and Beyond', JBL, 88.

Painter, John (1979) 'Johannine Symbols: A Case Study in Epistemology', *Journal of Theology for Southern Africa*, 27, pp. 26–41.

Patte, Daniel (1993) 'Structural Criticism', in S.L. Mckenzie and S.R. Haynes (eds) *To Each Its Own Meaning: An Introduction to Biblical Criticisms and their Application*, Geoffrey Chapman, London, pp. 153–70.

Peck, Chris (1988) 'Participatory Methods of Bible Study', *British Journal of Theological Education*, 2.2 (Winter 1988/9), pp. 31, 35.

Petersen, Norman (1985) *Rediscovering Paul*, Fortress Press, Philadelphia.

Potok, Chaim (1992) *The Gift of Asher Lev*, Penguin, Harmondsworth.

Pritchett, V.S. (ed.) (1981) *The Oxford Book of Short Stories*, Oxford University Press, Oxford.

Reeves, Marjorie (1992) 'A Speaking God', *Audenshaw Papers*, 138, February.

Richardson, Alan (1943) *How to Read the Bible – with Special Reference to the Old Testament*, Church Information Board, London.

Robbins, Vernon K. (1992) *Jesus the Teacher: A Socio-Rhetorical Interpretation of Mark*, Fortress Press, Philadelphia.

Smalley, Stephen S. (1994) *Thunder and Love*, Nelson Ward Ltd.

Spence, Basil (1962) *Phoenix at Coventry*, Geoffrey Bles, London.

Stevens, Wallace (1990) *Opus Posthumous*, Faber, London.

Stock, Augustine (1994) *The Method and Message of Matthew*, Liturgical Press, London.

Stowers, Stanley K. (1994) *A Rereading of Romans: Justice, Jews and Gentiles*, Yale University Press, London and New Haven, CT.

Streeter, B.H. (1924) *The Four Gospels*, Macmillan, London.

Taylor, Mark C. (1982) 'Deconstructing Theology', in Carl A. Raschke (ed.), *Deconstruction and Theology*, Crossroad, New York.

Taylor, Mark C. (1984) *Erring: A Postmodern A/theology*, University of Chicago Press, Chicago.

TeSelle, Sally (1975) *Speaking in Parables*, Fortress Press, Philadelphia/ SCM Press.

Theissen, Gerd (1987) *Psychological Aspects of Pauline Theology*, Fortress Press, Philadelphia.

Van Iersel, B. (1989) *Reading Mark*, Liturgical Press, London.

Weber, Hans-Ruedi (1981) *Experiments with Bible Study*, SCM Press, London.

Wells, David (1986) *The Penguin Dictionary of Curious and Interesting Numbers*, Penguin, Harmondsworth.

Whitman, Jon (1987) *Allegory: The Dynamics of an Ancient and Medieval Technique*, Clarendon Press.

Wiesel, Elie (1996) *A Beggar in Jerusalem*, Schocken Books.

Wink, Walter (1978) 'On Wrestling with God: Using Psychological Insights in Biblical Study', *Religion in Life*, 47.

Winnicott, D.W. (1965) *The Maturational Processes and the Facilitating Environment*, Hogarth, London.

Winter, Sara C. (1987) 'Paul's Letter to Philemon', *New Testament Studies*, vol. 33.

Wunderlich, Hans (1975) *The Secret of Crete*, Souvenir Press, London.

Young, Frances (1990) *The Art of Performance*, Darton Longman & Todd, London.

—— (1993) 'Allegory and the Ethics of Reading', in F. Watson (ed.) *The Open Text*, SCM Press, London, pp. 103–20.

Zimmer, Heinrich (1971) *The King and the Corpse – Tales of the Soul's Conquest of Evil*, Princeton University Press, Princeton, NJ.

Index

synagogues 101–2

Tablets of the Word 133–4
Tacitus 11, 12, 17–18
Talmud 143
Tanak *see* Old Testament ('Tanak')
Task Force for the Study of Narrative
   in the New Testament 26
Taylor, Mark C. 158
Taylor, Vincent 82
Ten Commandments 49, 132, 152–3
TeSelle, Sally 45
texts as slogans 129–36
Theissen, Gerd 111
Theodore 135
Theophilus 84
Theseus 155–6, 158–9
Thomas 135; Gospel of 46–8
Thucydides 12, 14, 15
Tiberius, Emperor 10, 11
Timothy 30
Trajan, Emperor 17
translation: accuracy 140–2;
   vocabulary 148
Travels of Marco Polo 55
Trinity, doctrine of 152
Triumph of Faith, The (Mitchison)
   27

Tyndale, William 140, 141
typology 115, 134–5

Uspensky, Boris 57

Van Iersel, Bas 41, 82, 85
Victor, Pope 151
Vitruvius 98

Wallace, Lewis 25
'wayside pulpits' 130
Weber, Hans-Ruedi 6
Wells, David 152
Whitman, Jon 124
Wiesel, Elie 45
Willett, Michael 111
Wink, Walter 6, 111
Winnicott, D.W. 107–8
Winter, Sara C. 32, 34
women (in New Testament) 41
Wunderlich, Hans 155

Xenophon of Ephesus 18
Xenophon (historian) 86

Young, Frances 123–8

Zimmer, Heinrich 156